celebrating
BIRD

celebrating

B·I·R·D

The Triumph of
CHARLIE PARKER

Gary Giddins

BEECH TREE BOOKS
A QUILL EDITION
New York

For the grand destruction one must be worthy.
—ELIZABETH HARDWICK

Some would hold . . . that music has some contribution to make to the
cultivation of our minds and to the growth of moral wisdom.
—ARISTOTLE

I know noble accents
And lucid, inescapable rhythms;
But I know, too,
That the blackbird is involved
In what I know.
—WALLACE STEVENS

FOR DEBORAH EVE

Produced by Toby Byron/Multiprises

Grateful acknowledgment is made for permission to quote lines from "Thirteen Ways of
Looking at a Blackbird." Copyright 1923 and renewed 1951 by Wallace Stevens.
Reprinted from THE COLLECTED POEMS OF WALLACE STEVENS by Wallace
Stevens, by permission of Alfred A. Knopf, Inc.

It is the policy of William Morrow and Company, Inc., and its imprints and affiliates, recog-
nizing the importance of preserving what has been written, to print the books we publish
on acid-free paper, and we exert our best efforts to that end.

Library of Congress Catalog Card Number: 86-61275

ISBN: 0-688-05950-3

Book design by Kathleen Westray and Ed Sturmer, Design and Printing Productions

Printed in the United States of America

6 7 8 9 10

The word "book" is said to derive from *boka,* or beech.
The beech tree has been the patron tree of writers since ancient times and
represents the flowering of literature and knowledge.

Contents

Acknowledgments

MY FIRST DEBT is to Toby Byron, who asked me to write an extended essay on Charlie Parker and left me free to go about it in my own fashion. Toby is responsible for the book's physical beauty. He rounded up the photographs and presided over every detail of the design. Ever scrupulous and resourceful, he also proved a better than fair detective in locating obscure phone numbers and tracking down useful bits of information.

My second first debt is to Stanley Crouch, friend and colleague, who has been working since 1982 on an exhaustive study of Parker's life and art. Having read several chapters, I have no doubt it will be a milestone in the literature of American music. In what was surely an unusual if not unprecedented act of scholarly comradeship, Stanley made all of his research available to me so that I could "get it right." His extensive interviews with Rebecca Parker Davis convinced me that she knew the story I wanted to tell.

My third first debt is to Rebecca Parker Davis, Charlie's childhood sweetheart and first wife, whom no biographer had even contacted before Stanley. From the first moments we spoke, her candor, enthusiasm, and vivid memory confirmed my instinct to look closely at Charlie Parker's apprentice years. How, I wondered, did the unprepossessing child of Addie and Charles Parker, Sr., come to be the lengendary Bird of the years 1945–55, when he revolutionized the music of his time? Rebecca never hesitated to call whenever she remembered another incident that might unravel the puzzle.

The Rashomon-like complexity of Parker's life is especially acute as regards his remarkably diverse and devoted wives, legal or common-law. I've concentrated on Rebecca's perspective, not only because of my interest in his early years and her concern with nailing down details, but because it has been ignored in the past. Indeed, in Ross Russell's *Bird Lives!*, which is often more roman à clef than biography, even her name is misspelled. Of the other wives, Geraldine Scott is deceased; Doris Sydnor's view is given in Robert Reisner's *Bird: The Legend of Charlie Parker;* Chan Richardson's is told by Russell (she wrote an introduction to the French edition of *Bird Lives!*), and in the massive photojournal, *To Bird with Love* (compiled with Francis Paudras), and her as yet unfinished memoir, *Life in E-Flat.* I've tried not to repeat material from my own previous writings. For additional comments on Parker's recordings and an account of his association with Red Rodney and others, the reader might consult my *Riding on a Blue Note.*

It is a measure of the general esteem in which Parker is held that so many people—musicians, friends, collectors, Bird-lovers all—contributed to this project. Almost all the biographical material is drawn from or confirmed by original research, including that of Crouch and the oral history archive at the Institute of Jazz Studies at Rutgers University. In the end, I had more information than I could use, but everyone with whom I spoke contributed to my sense of Parker.

My thanks to Chan Parker, Jay McShann, Buddy Tate, Gerry Mulligan, John Lewis, Big Nick Nicholas, Buddy DeFranco, Al Cohn, Roland Hanna, Ed Shaughnessy, Dizzy Gillespie, Phil Woods, Joe Newman, Muhal Richard Abrams, Thad Jones, Leonard Feather, Dr. H., William Dufty, Bevan Dufty, Red Rodney, Dexter Gordon, Benny Carter, Earl Coleman, Woody Herman, Maxwell T. Cohen, Ted Curson, Hank Jones, Johnny Griffin, David Amram, Don Schlitten, Dan Morgenstern, Rolf Ljungquist, Gil Evans, Lee Konitz, and, hail and farewell, Bob Reisner, Budd Johnson, Mary Lou Williams, Al Haig, and Art Pepper. For research assistance of various kinds, I'm grateful to Angela Gaudioso, Norman Saks, Ira Berger, Steve Futterman, and Burt Korall. All jazz historians would be diminished without the Institute of Jazz Studies, as administered by Dan Morgenstern, Ed Berger, and Marie Griffin; and the Schomburg Center for Black Studies, to which Ernie Smith has extended his invaluable library of films. My thanks to Brian Swann, who helped untangle my metaphors; my agent Emilie Jacobson; various members of the Giddins, Halper, and Rothchild families; and Jim Landis of Beech Tree Books for his interest and, yes yes yes, patience. Above all, a toast to Charlie Parker. Ever since I first heard an album called *Bird Symbols*, twenty three years ago, his music has been a bottomless source of pleasure, and a faithful paradigm of cultural endeavor.

G.G.

In addition to Dan, Ed, and Marie at the Institute of Jazz Studies; Ernie Smith, Don Schlitten, and those already thanked, I would like to thank Ken Poston of the Kansas City Jazz Society, Robert Dobrish, Bob Parent, Bill Gottlieb, Frank Driggs, Francis Paudras, and all of the photographers and collectors who so graciously shared their materials, and Steve Alpert, Patty Dryden, and Jane Meara.

A special thanks must go to Ed Sturmer and Kathleen Westray for work above and beyond the call of duty, and for bringing it in on time.

In Germany, Walter Lautz; and in France, Paulette and Agnes at Magnum; Thierry Trombert, Jean-Pierre Leloir, François Chauvelot (Club Hot Brass, Celony), Hôtel Moderne of Aix; and most of all Chan and Aimée for sharing their home and Bird (I'm forever indebted); and Anne Bournazelle for Les Baux, the Camargue, and Antibes. And, yes, Jim Landis for his commitment and support.

This is for Lloyd Byron and Rick Saylor, who listened first.

T.R.B.

BIRD LIVES!

T HE WITNESS to his death heard a clap of thunder at the moment of Charlie Parker's passing. The companion of his last years remains in spiritual contact with him after more than thirty years. His childhood sweetheart and first wife continues to hear his music as nothing more or less than the "story of our lives together." Such indications of veneration and awe, shot through by an unmistakable religious symbology, suggest the extent to which Parker's posthumous life is clouded with romance. Deification did not begin with his death. Parker, who enjoyed remarkably little public recognition in life, was nonetheless attended by disciples and hagiographers. Many musicians, a few critics, and a coterie of enthusiasts—most of them drawn from the tight-knit, defensive world of jazz—were inspired by his music to the often voluble rapture that finds comfort in the elaborations of myth.

Parker's status as a prophet was largely inadvertent, a by-product of his self-acknowledged destiny to become "a great musician." As an apprentice in Kansas City jazz circles, he got off to a slow start. He impressed fellow apprentices with little more than his confidence and determination; others thought him lazy, obdurate, and spoiled. But the young man was favored with supernatural abilities, and the tempo of his life quickened soon enough. Resolve gave way to obsession and a desire to succeed equaled only by a vertiginous desire to fail. He hurled himself at the gates, falsifying his age to gain entry into the most competitive nightclubs, daring Kansas City to reject him, and maximizing every rejection as a stimulus for new feats. He forged ahead with astonishing assurance. At sixteen, he was laughed off a bandstand; at seventeen, he made converts—including Jay McShann, a stranger in town, who eventually offered him the chance to reject Kansas City. The fledgling, who many years later would answer a query about his religious affiliation by declaring himself

Opposite page: Charlie Parker, Detroit, 1950.

"a devout musician," was too conscious of his genius, too possessed of pride, too much the product of racial repression and maternal sanction not to suspect that a larger world awaited him—a world he could recast in his own image.

It's no surprise to learn that Parker was embarrassed by the insipid onomatopoeia *bebop*, which got tarred to modern jazz and which survives his scorn. He never proselytized for modernism in any guise. Impatient with those who attempted to stampede him into aesthetic cubbyholes, he jousted with critics—celebrating the traditions of jazz in one interview (*Down Beat*, 1948) and dismissing those traditions in another (*Down Beat*, 1949). Asked to distinguish between his music and that of his predecessors, however, he invariably demurred: "It's just music. It's trying to play clean and looking for the pretty notes" (1949). His willigness to let people draw their own conclusions is suggested in his one surviving television appearance, when he disdainfully tells the dotty emcee, "They say music speaks louder than words, so we'd rather voice our opinion that way." Everyone agrees that he knew his own worth and had neither the need nor the desire to politick on behalf of a new movement. On the contrary, he kept himself humble with an attentive enthusiasm for those modernists—Stravinsky, Hindemith, Schönberg, Bartok—who were skilled in the compositional techniques he coveted. Yet at twenty five, he was the acknowledged leader of a new music; at thirty, his brilliance was recognized by musicians around the world; at thirty four, when he died, he was regarded as an elder statesman who had yet to be superceded by his descendants. No sooner was he buried—in Easter season—than the graffiti appeared: *Bird lives!*

Parker's followers dogged his footsteps, often armed with tape recorders to preserve his improvised performances (but not those of his accompanists, most of whom also have claims on posterity). Some put words to his music. One such lyricist, a singer who called himself King Pleasure, made a profession of the practice and paid Parker the dubious but canonical tribute of predicting his death in his words to "Parker's Mood." Parker sought allied musicians (and could be stern with those who failed to make the grade), but he did not seek followers and tended to be contemptuous of idolizers. He had little use for cult foppery—beret, beard, jive talk—or cult arrogance. If he seems to have attracted converts rather than mere fans or imitators, the reason is obvious. Parker was the only jazz musician since Louis Armstrong whose innovations demanded a comprehensive reassessment of all the elements of jazz.

It's natural for a saxophonist to influence saxophonists, or a drummer drummers. But Parker, like Armstrong before him, engineered a total shift in the jazz aesthetic. The autodidactic

Louis Armstrong, Chicago, 1930.

At the Three Deuces, 1948: (left to right) Tommy Potter, Charlie Parker, Max Roach (hidden behind Charlie Parker), Miles Davis, Duke Jordan.

country boy from Kansas City brought modernism to jazz, and forced players on every instrument to face their worst fears or realize their most prized aspirations in his music. Established players satisfied with approved jazz styles encountered not only new levels of harmony, melody, and rhythm in Parker's work—all of which evolved from precedents easily found in classic jazz—but an iconoclastic sensibility that threatened to undermine generally accepted standards of excellence. Younger players were more open to the shock of recognition that, to paraphrase Melville, binds not only the community of geniuses but that of apprentice artists impatient to express their own powers in a world paralyzed with orthodoxy. Small wonder, then, that so many musicians of Parker's generation (and not a few elders) tell of how he changed their lives with a way of playing music they scarcely imagined. The witnesses are many, but the language is similar:

JAY McSHANN: When I first came to Kansas City, I went to all the clubs to meet all the musicians. So one night I stopped . . . .

Buddy De Franco, Loew's Kings Theater, Brooklyn, New York, March 24, 1952.

Opposite page: (clockwise) Billy Bauer, Eddie Safranski, Charlie Parker, Lennie Tristano, RCA Studios, New York, January 1949, at a recording session for the Metronome All Stars.

in a club and Bird was blowing. That was in 1937, and he was *playing,* and you know the first time you hear Bird, you *hear* it—you've got to hear it. I asked him, "Say, man, where are you from? You don't play like anybody else in Kansas City." He said, "Well, I've been down in the Ozarks with George Lee's band. It's hard to get musicians to go down there, because it's quiet and musicians like to be where the action is, but I wanted to do some woodshedding so I went down there with George. That's probably the reason you think I sound different."

DIZZY GILLESPIE: I had a friend, Buddy Anderson, who played good trumpet with Jay McShann, and we'd jam together in Kansas City. He wanted me to hear this saxophone player, but I wasn't too interested because I'd been hearing Don Byas, Lester Young, Chu Berry, Coleman Hawkins, and Ben Webster, and I said, "Not another saxophone player!" Until I heard him. Jesus! Knocked me off my feet. We played all day that day. . . .

RED RODNEY: Dizzy kept telling me about this saxophone player I had to hear . . . he took me up to New York with him and I met Charlie Parker. When I heard him play I near fell out the window. Oh, my God! Everything came together at one time. I knew then. I knew where it was and who was it and what I had to do.

BUDDY DE FRANCO: He was just three years older than me, but he seemed so much more mature and older . . . when I got to know him I got to realize that he was more than just an innovator and a musician. He was a deep, extremely knowledgeable person, though self-taught. I don't think he had professional training and teaching, but his fingers were perfect. His technique was just *perfect*—as though he had years of schooling. To me it's incredible that he's the one person in jazz who influenced the entire jazz world. Every bit of it.

JOE NEWMAN: Jay McShann had his band at the Savoy Ballroom and Rudy Williams, a well-known alto player at the time, said, "Come on with me, man, I want you to meet this alto player." He introduced me to Bird and the first time I heard him play I couldn't believe it, because he was doing something different from what everybody else was doing, and it was obvious his style was going to force things in another direction.

THAD JONES: I was in the army on an island called Guam, traveling with a GI show. There were about six of us, all in our tent, preparing for the evening and listening to the radio, and all of a sudden Dizzy comes on playing "Shaw Nuff" with Charlie Parker. And, you know, I can't describe what went on in that tent. We went out of our minds! . . . It was the newness and the impact of that sound, and the technique. It was some-

thing we were probably trying to articulate ourselves and just didn't know how. And Dizzy and Bird came along and did it. They spoke our minds.

Of course, Parker's travail as prophetic genius, accepted only by a coterie in his own country, was hardly as unambiguous as that of the traditional romance. Nor, tragically, were his converts satisfied with imitating just his music. The usual tale of the exceptionally gifted and sensitive young artist who is emboldened by despair and suffering, and ultimately overcomes self-doubt and public indifference, is too conventional, too perfunctory (perhaps too European) to suit Charlie Parker. Parker achieved his hipster sainthood in part by transcending, in word if not in deed, a full measure of Augustinian vices. If Parker's career was a frantic quest for musical fulfillment, it was continuously detoured by self-destructive impulses so gargantuan that they also became the stuff of legend. The bop king had another, by no means secret, identity as the junkie king, and many votaries unable to get close to him musically were eager to share the communion of drugs. "Do as I say, not as I do," Parker warned friends when they asked about that part of his life. He kept it private, refusing to partake with those he respected, at least until they were as far gone as he was. Despite his warnings, many persisted in the sometimes fatal belief that Parker drew part of his seemingly inexhaustible greatness from teaspoons of white powder.

Disconcerted commentators can be forgiven the inclination to link Parker's gluttonies to racism and an absent father. Still, something basic in Parker's individuality resists the familiar simplifications of fast-Freud analyses. The hugeness, majesty, and authority of this man are diminished when the culpability for his downfall is removed from his shoulders and placed on those of an uncomprehending commonalty. Racist and philistine societies are all alike; every artist is unique. The shift in blame from Parker to the mass tethers him to the very prosaicness his art so unequivocally counters. Always one step ahead of the mob, he cut himself down before they could. Still, it must be emphasized that as a black man in mid-twentieth-century America, Parker suffered more than personal injustices. He also endured a constant debilitating slander against his art. Minority citizens healthily buffered by their own communities do not look to the oppressive majority for a sense of identity. The artist, however, seeks recognition in the community of artists, which defies, or ought to defy, the conventionalism, mediocrity, and pettiness that are inseparable from race and nationalism. In that community, a far worse fate than neglect is acknowledgement followed by expulsion for lack of an acceptable pedigree. By all accounts, Parker

Opposite page: Roy Haynes and Charlie Parker at the Open Door, January 1953.

. . . .

15

(Left to right) Billy Bauer, Eddie Safranski, Charlie
Parker, Lennie Tristano: the rhythm section for the
Metronome All Stars recording session, January 1949.

· · · · · · · · · · · ·

Charlie Parker and Red Rodney listen to Dizzy Gillespie and Clyde Lombardi at the Club Downbeat, New York City, 1948.

could not be cowed by the insanity of white supremacism. But the frustration he experienced on behalf of his music was lifelong and stifling.

Parker was bred in one of the richest musical communities in American history: Kansas City in the 1930s. In addition to constant access to dozens of the most individual and accomplished musicians in the country, he could hear the rest of the world's best jazz musicians on records and radio. As a provisionally popular music, jazz wasn't merely available; it was virtually inescapable. But partly because of its popularity, it was also reputed to be lacking in seriousness: a folk music at best, a fad for adolescents at worst. The combination of Jim Crow racism and the public's inability to distinguish genuine achievement from meritricious imitation invariably favored the exposure of white bands. Since the most successful of those bands diluted their music with trite novelties and feeble showmanship, jazz itself was widely construed to be a low art. In Europe, Japan, and elsewhere, jazz was celebrated as a vital music. In the United States, jazz was confined to gin mills and dance halls. It was practically banned from concert halls until 1938, when—significantly enough—the Benny Goodman band played Carnegie Hall, and from conservatories for much longer. It was ignored by most classical music critics, and still is.

When he died, in 1955, Charlie Parker was arguably the most

influential musician in the country. Jazz musicians copied him so shamelessly that the pianist Lennie Tristano made an oft-quoted remark to the effect that Parker could have invoked plagiarism laws. On more than one occasion, Charles Mingus made a show of firing his musicians on the bandstand for relying on Parker clichés. Studio musicians were no less mesmerized by Parker's ideas, as witness the wholesale use of bebop harmonies and melodic figures (once considered terrifyingly complex) as fodder for movie and television scores, as well as arrangements for pop and rock-and-roll records. It's doubtful that the host of the *Ed Sullivan Show* knew his entrances were cued by Parkeresque phrases, or that moviegoers who watched *The Helen Morgan Story* realized the 1920s torch singer was crooning to 1950s bop licks, or that kids dancing to "The Hucklebuck" recognized the melody as Parker's "Now's the Time." Forty years after Parker and Gillespie popularized Latin rhythms, salsa bands continue to feature solos played in their styles. As Parker's influence extended into the repertory of "legitimate" ensembles—for examples, David Amram symphonies with passages for Parker-styled improvisations and John Lewis fugues and ballets—Gunther Schuller coined the term Third Stream to suggest a new pluralism inspired in large measure by Parker's music. Indeed, his impact

Dizzy Gillespie leading his Orchestra, c. 1948.

transcended music. In the 1950s, numerous novelists, poets, and painters cited him with metaphorical urgency, often as the embodiment of a psychic breakthrough.

Yet the various rewards with which a society pays tribute to its artists were denied Parker. The academic musical world, notwithstanding individual admirers such as Varese, never knew him. Countless jazz and popular performers who worshipped him achieved a renown that persistently eluded Parker. In fact, the cultural racism that sneers at jazz had sniped at his heels from the moment he obtained a saxophone: he never had the option of studying at the two conservatories in Kansas City because neither accepted black students. When, at the peak of his influence, *Life* ran an article on bop, Parker wasn't discussed. When *Time* cast about for a cover story on the new jazz, it turned to a white musician with a "classical" education, Dave Brubeck—a slight that especially riled Parker. If the mainstream press ignored him, the jazz press wasn't much more perspicacious. He won few jazz polls, even when all the winners reflected his guidance. The best-known jazz club of the era (Birdland) was named for him, yet in concert appearances with Gillespie he was usually billed second and in smaller type. When he died in New York City, where he'd lived most of his adult life and achieved his greatest successes, a minority of local newspapers published obituaries. Of those that acknowledged his passing, only *The New York Post* got his age right (the others gave fifty-three) or attempted to suggest his impact on the music of his time. Two papers failed to learn his first name and buried him as Yardbird Parker.

Posterity made up for that neglect in a hurry, not with an accurate rendering of facts, but with a rush of memories, many of them self-serving, a mad pastiche of discipleship and true love. "I knew him better than anyone," is the most frequent pledge a Parker biographer hears. But the fairest warning he can expect is that of the far from dispassionate observer who said, "You will talk to a million people and you will hear of a million Charlie Parkers." One wonders if it is even possible to peel away the Charlie Parker created in death by family and disciples, hagiographers and voyeurs, and if so to what purpose? Would a Charlie Parker reduced to life size be more easily apprehended, understood, and admired, or even closer to the truth, than the one of legend? The one irreducible fact of his existence is his genius, which will not cater to the routine explanations of psychologists, sociologists, anthropologists, or musicologists. But a basic ordering of facts, as best they can be adduced with limited resources in the face of conflicting claims (most of them plenary), may complement the music of Charlie Parker and engage the imagination of listeners who know the ravishing pleasures of his art.

Opposite page: Birdland and the Bandbox, Broadway near 52nd Street, New York City, January 1953.

YOUTH

CHARLES PARKER, JR., was born August 29, 1920, in Kansas City, Kansas, during a bitterly contested presidential election. In previous weeks, Senator Warren G. Harding of Ohio had emerged as the compromise candidate for the Republicans, with Governor Calvin Coolidge of Massachusetts filling out the ticket. *The New York Times*, in an extraordinary front-page editorial, accused the convention of "cowardice and imbecility" and argued "we must go back to Franklin Pierce if we would seek a President who measures down to [Harding's] political stature." The Democrats settled on Ohio's Governor James Cox and Secretary of the Navy Franklin D. Roosevelt. The Republican landslide foretokened an era of unexampled corruption, exceeding party affiliations. Within three years the nation learned of the administration's illicit dealings in oil reserves. Even before that, numerous municipalities had fallen into the hands of venal politicians and their gangster sponsors, for 1920 was also the year the Volsted Act took effect. During its tenure (1920–33), legitimate businessmen were barred from selling, manufacturing, or distributing alcoholic beverages. No other minority group would ever get so generous a boost from Congress as organized crime received from Senator Volsted, and no community would plunge into the trough more extravagantly than Kansas City, Missouri, just across the Kaw River from Charlie Parker's birthplace.

The United States was experiencing birth pangs of various sorts in 1920. The Republican victory was in part a repudiation of Wilsonian idealism, which was widely blamed for the country's entanglement in the Great War. Isolationists who spurned the League of Nations and demanded reparations from Germany succeeded only in helping to starve a bellicose nation and insure another war. Few noticed, but in 1920 Hitler founded the Nazi party. America was more concerned with domestic bolshevism, unionism, and anarchy—Sacco and Vanzetti were arrested that

Opposite page: Charlie Parker and the King alto he favored when he began playing with an ensemble of strings, c. 1950.

Charlie Parker and his half brother, John, nicknamed Ikey, Kansas City, Kansas.

year. A few new novels—*Main Street, The Age of Innocence, This Side of Paradise, Painted Veils* (which was banned as obscene)—indicated a growing impatience with provincial values. And a new American music called jazz was successfully touring Europe. Black jazz musicians could not yet record, however, and the hit songs that greeted the infant Charlie Parker included "I Love the Land of Old Black Joe," "Alabama Moon," "My Little Bimbo Down on the Bamboo Isle," and "Whatcha Gonna Do When There Ain't No Jazz?" Curiously, a song called "Cherokee" also made its debut, though it was entirely unrelated to the one Parker favored. On the other hand, 1920 was the year women were given the vote and a cultural renaissance took hold in Harlem. Massive demonstrations by black soldiers, the theatrical success of Eugene O'Neill's *The Emperor Jones*, and the first convention of Marcus Garvey's Universal Negro Improvement Association all contributed to the renewed awareness of a nation within the nation.

The Parkers lived at 852 Freeman Street, an intimate suburban neighborhood quite unlike the glittery city about to burgeon in Missouri. Charles Parker Sr., born in Mississippi and bred in Memphis, drifted to Kansas while touring as a dancer and singer on the T.O.B.A. circuit, a substandard chain of theaters organized in 1911, which maintained a harsh dominion over black vaudeville. (The acronym stood for Theater Owners Booking Association, but performers considered it Tough on Black Asses.) His sallow coloring set off dark brown eyes, and he wore his hair slicked and parted on the side. Parker drank heavily, though rarely at home, since his wife did not tolerate liquor in the house. His alcoholism eventually precipitated their separation, by which time he had gone to work as a chef on the Pullman line, a job that kept him away from home.

Charlie Parker, Kansas City, Kansas.

Charlie's mother was the former Addie Boxley,* a broad-shouldered, deep-bosomed woman, who many thought beautiful and all found steely and dignified. Her family came from Muskogee, Oklahoma, and her part-Choctaw ancestry was readily apparent in prominent cheek bones and thin lips. She wore her gray-streaked hair long, plaited atop her head in two big buns; she favored dangling earrings and wore glasses that seemed to magnify her obsidian eyes, which her future daughter-in-law, Rebecca Ruffin, says, "could cut you to the quick." The family was completed by an older half-brother John, known as Ikey, who was Mr. Parker's son from a previous liaison with an Italian woman.

Addie sent Charlie to a Catholic school because it was reputed to be better than the public school, but she probably regretted her decision when he brought orthodox teachings into her Baptist home. In any case, she soon enrolled him in the nonsectarian Charles Sumner Elementary School. A quiet boy and the focus of his mother's life, Charlie was well behaved, studious, and apparently content. He played with Ikey and a neighborhood friend, and rarely spoke of his father who was usually on the road. During the late twenties, Charles Sr. left for good, taking his older son with him. He had hoped to find work as a dancer across the river in Missouri, but as the Depression neared, vaudeville was on the way out. He stayed with the Pullman line, traveling through the Midwest, and Charlie saw him only a couple of times after that. In a 1950 interview with Marshall Stearns, he spoke briefly but with an unmistakable tone of defensiveness about his father: "Sure was a well-tutored guy," he said, "spoke two or three languages."

In a 1949 interview, Parker said he was seven when the family moved to Missouri; his biographers have assumed that the putative 1927 move involved Mr. Parker. But it seems certain that Charles Sr. had departed some time before Addie and the boy relocated. Moreover, Rebecca recalls seeing his diploma from Charles Sumner, which indicates that the move took place in 1931. They settled in a traditional two-story frame house in the heart of the black district of the more populous Kansas City, and Addie worked as a charwoman for Western Union, cleaned houses, took in laundry, and rented the top floor to boarders. She spoiled the boy utterly, dressing him in made-to-order suits (short pants, of course) and refusing to let him deliver papers or do any other kind of work. In the sometimes misleading account (especially as it pertains to other women in Parker's life) she gave Robert Reisner, Addie boasted: "Whenever he needed anything,

Addie Parker, date unknown.

*Mrs. Parker's maiden name is a mystery. The Ruffins, who were close to the Parkers (they are buried in adjoining plots, the former Rebecca Ruffin points out), insist on Boxley or Boxely. A birth certificate for Charlie Parker, certified in 1958, gives her name as Bailey; and Charlie's passport application says Boyley or Bayley.

Charlie Parker, age 16.

all he had to do was call, and it was there. That's what I worked for and what I lived for, that boy." In the Stearns interview, Parker was fairly animated on the subject of his mother: "She's *very* much alive . . . she's sixty-two and just graduated from nursing school. She don't look it or act it—she's spryer than me . . . she takes good care of herself, she owns her own home . . . very well situated."

The home he referred to, the one Addie bought and lived in for the rest of her life, was down the street from the one she rented when she and Charlie first moved to Missouri. Located at 1516 Olive Street, the house in which Charlie came of age was a short walk from the nightclubs and dance halls where a new style of jazz was being born. There was a swing on the front porch, and eventually a piano and victrola in the parlor. Downstairs Addie

The remains of the house at 1516 Olive.
Opposite page: Lawrence "88" Keyes, 1945.

had a room near the kitchen which separated her from the large room where Charlie slept, warmed in winter by a potbellied stove. His mother claimed he did exceptionally well at Crispus Attucks Public School, but there's some question as to whether he actually graduated. If he graduated from grade school in Kansas, the only reason for him to enroll in a Missouri grade school would be the age difference that can force a child to repeat a year. Charlie, already highly sensitive, might have experienced that enrollment as a humiliation. Rebecca, who graduated from Attucks in 1931, doesn't recall seeing him in attendance, though at least one teacher remembers him as bright and eager to please. In any case, something happened to Charlie Parker in the year before seventh grade that effected a sea change.

A strangely different Charlie registered for Lincoln High School in 1932. The impeccably dressed, ingratiating, and fussed-over child was now an incorrigible truant. Once again he was forced to repeat a grade, his freshman year, but this time the only reason was his inadequacy in class. Parker often said that he had begun to dissipate at twelve and started using hard drugs at fifteen—an exaggeration, as will be seen, but one that underscores the trauma of those years. The mystery is compounded by the paralyzing speed with which he shuffled off his childhood and found a spiritual home in jazz. If Parker was destined to become a prominent musician, as he and at least one close friend believed, there were few early signs. His first flirtation with music was as fleeting as that of most children who ask for music lessons. At thirteen, he expressed enthusiasm for the sound of Rudy Vallee's saxophone on the radio, and his ever-obliging mother bought him a used and unplayable alto for forty-five dollars. After she invested a larger sum to repair it, his interest waned and the instrument was loaned to a friend.

Writing of Lautrec, Aldous Huxley observed, "Up to the age of ten (provided of course that his teachers don't interfere) practically every child paints like a genius. Fifteen years later the chances of his still painting like a genius are about four hundred thousand to one." Charlie's artistic ripening reversed the usual process. Not until he reached fifteen did the rebel apprentice display an aptitude for music, and even then his talent seemed negligible. During his second try as a freshman, Charlie was encouraged to join the school's marching band by its locally celebrated bandmaster, Alonzo Lewis, whose students already numbered several of Kansas City's professional musicians. At first he was assigned an alto horn, but he switched to baritone horn as soon as the student who played it graduated.

Charlie quickly realized the limitations of the cumbersome brass instrument and grew bored with the stilted parts written for

it. Addie thought it looked "heavy and funny coiled around him with just his head sticking out." Yet the baritone served the purpose of bringing him into contact with the older kids who played music and were charmed by his questions and enthusiasm. At around the same time he began associating with Mr. Lewis's prize pupils, notably pianist Lawrence Keyes who had a band called the Deans of Swing, Charlie retrieved his alto and started practicing with a vengeance. For nearly two years, nothing about the boy's playing suggested much potential. Only the degree of his obsession, a burning faith that enlarged his gaze beyond customary responsibilities, begged notice. He taught himself as best he could, soliciting help from anyone who might be able to teach him, but he attended school periodically, chiefly to play in the band. He stayed out late, sometimes overnight. Addie looked the other way when he disappeared, although she forbade him from walking into the combat zone around Twelfth Street, where many of the best musicians could be heard.

Charlie's discovery of Kansas City's musical riches and, indeed, his mother's move to that city coincided with the rise to

George E. Lee Singing Novelty Orchestra: (left to right) Thurston "Sox" Harris, Bob Garner, Charles Bass, George E. Lee, Chester Clark, Julia Lee, Abe Price, Kansas City, Missouri, 1929.

Benny Moten's Band: (left to right) Jimmy Rushing, Jack Washington, Woodie Walder, Count Basie, Leroy Berry, Bus Moten, Eddie Durham, Willie McWashington, Vernon Page, Thamon Hayes, Harlan Leonard, Ed Lewis, Booker Washington, Bennie Moten, behind Old Folks Home, Kansas City, Missouri, 1929.

power of the infamous Tom Pendergast. Born in St. Joseph, Missouri, in 1872, Pendergast was a vain, muscle-bound ward-heeler who affected a rakish derby and prized his ability at fisticuffs. His family had long been involved in the distribution of liquor, so when the Volsted Act went into effect he took over a cement company as a front. His ability to deliver the Democratic vote plus the backing of organized crime guaranteed his rise to power. As councilman, he appointed a friend as city manager and by 1931 controlled Kansas City, which became known as Tom's Town. The Depression stopped at his door, while businesses like gambling, loan sharking, prostitution, narcotics, and extortion thrived. When Pretty Boy Floyd found things too hot in Oklahoma, he lit out for Tom's Town. So did the Sicilian mafia, which established its midwestern axis there rather than Chicago, where the Neapolitan Al Capone governed. Naturally, entertainment also flourished. The clubs and dance halls operated day and night, and the best musicians in the country were attracted as much by the competitive atmosphere of excellence besting excellence as by the possiblilities for employment.

Andy Kirk came from Denver, Count Basie from New Jersey, Mary Lou Williams from Pittsburgh. But most of the major jazz players traveled a much shorter distance, from Texas, Oklahoma, and Missouri itself. Many of them had played in territory bands, and Kansas City was the richest territory of all, the Las

Hot Lips Page, Charlie Parker, Paris, 1949.
Opposite page: Charlie Parker and Gene Ramey,
Wichita, Kansas, 1940.

Vegas of its day. Among those who passed through, many of them
ripe for the picking of eastern promoters, were Jimmy Rushing,
Lester Young, Eddie Durham, Hot Lips Page, Jo Jones, Gus
Johnson, Walter Page, Ben Webster, Herschel Evans, Dick Wil-
son, Gene Ramey, Eddie Barefield, Charlie Christian, Buster
Smith, Buddy Tate, Henry Bridges, Jay McShann, Joe Turner,
Pete Johnson, Jesse Price, Budd Johnson, Bennie Moten, Julia
Lee, Herman Walder, Tadd Dameron, Harlan Leonard, and Fred
Beckett. And if that wasn't enough, nationally famous touring
bands—those of Duke Ellington, Fletcher Henderson, Jimmie
Lunceford, and Cab Calloway—brought Coleman Hawkins, Chu
Berry, Johnny Hodges, Barney Bigard, Willie Smith, Dizzy Gilles-
pie, and numerous other virtuosi to town.

The milieu that the teenage Charlie Parker made his own was
soaked in the blues, and lavish with scorching rhythms and star-
tling improvisational conceits. Playing absurdly long hours,

Rebecca Parker, January 1937.
Opposite page: Charlie Parker at Billy Berg's, Hollywood, California, 1946.

sometimes around the clock, what with breakfast dates, matinees, dances, and after-hours clubs, the bands specialized in fashioning head arrangements, which were invented on the bandstand through the communal mastery of a lexicon of riffs. Riffs—punching phrases, short and rhythmic, that picked up momentum with repetition—were the building blocks of big-band arrangements and the basis for much improvisation. When the Kansas City sound spread across the country, many of those improvised scores were formalized and recorded. (Basie's "One O'Clock Jump," for example.) Like New Orleans and Chicago before it, Kansas City was a hotbed for creative music financed by racketeers with no interest in music. Some thugs forced bands to work free weeks just to flaunt their power. Yet when Pendergast went to jail for tax fraud in 1938, the Kansas City era in jazz began to fade.

Charlie's awakening to music was accompanied by another awakening. Rebecca Ellen Ruffin vividly recalls the first time she saw him, on April 10, 1934, when she, her mother, brother, and five sisters moved into the Parker home. Until her parents divorced, the Ruffin family had lived several blocks away. On the day they brought their belongings to 1516 Olive, toting them up the staircase to settle in the second-floor rooms, Charlie and Addie stood against the lower banister. Rebecca felt his eye on her and imagined that he'd never seen so many girls before, and that he'd singled her out. She noticed he wore knickers, which seemed odd for a boy as big as he was, and made no effort to help them carry their bags. "You want to know about Charlie Parker? I'll tell you about Charlie Parker—he was *lazy!*" she says, but with an endearing tone her mother could never comprehend. Fanny Ruffin, an imposing, principled woman ("we were religious, book-learning people," Rebecca says), saw her worst suspicions about Charlie's good-for-nothing ways confirmed in his habitual absence from school and his predilection for shooting marbles with a friend, Sterling Bryant, by the side of the house. She called him an alley rat and expressed displeasure at the friendship that swiftly developed between Charlie and her children, especially the daughter he quietly eyed that first day. Rebecca was an uncommonly pretty girl, with fair skin and a slinky figure; a few years later people would tell her she looked like a young Lena Horne. Born February 23, 1920, she was Charlie's age and she took to him right away.

As the families grew close, they discovered they had much in common. Each had lived in Kansas (the Ruffins traveled to the Midwest from Memphis) and had Indian blood, the Ruffins more than the Parkers. Addie was one-quarter Choctaw and Charles Sr.'s stock was less easily defined, while Fannie was half-Chero-

kee and half-English and her husband, Marcus W. Ruffin, an insurance salesman with a dark, ruddy complexion, was Indian and Negro. The Parkers and Ruffins lived as one big family, with Charlie increasingly the focus of attention; the other children adopted him as a sibling. Parker's biographers have assumed Rebecca was older than Charlie, presumably because she graduated from Lincoln High in 1935. But in the Kansas City school system, you went to grade school until you were eleven or twelve, and required only four years of secondary school for a diploma—allowing for graduation at fifteen or sixteen. "Extra years" were optional. Charlie would have graduated in 1935 as well had he progressed each term. Rebecca believes he was on the verge of dropping out for good when he was forced to repeat his freshman year. The only reason he continued as long as he did was the pleasure he took in walking to and from school with Rebecca and two of her sisters: "Charlie enjoyed walking with the three girls—seemed like he had a family."

Charlie was a lonely boy, a mama's boy. Addie insisted he wear made-to-order suits to high school and gave him anything he wanted. "He didn't have to do anything because Parky took care of him," Rebecca says, using Addie's nickname given her by a cousin, Hattie Lee, who subsequently moved into the house. Yet Ikey was never around, and other than Sterling, the boy he played marbles with, Charlie didn't seem to have any friends. Addie had a boyfriend, a deacon who visited twice a week and disappeared with her into the bedroom—much to Fannie's consternation. The son would sit in the living room, waiting and looking dejected, while the Ruffin children, congregating around the piano, tried to divert his attention. Rebecca took a job in the library, and Charlie, though his own attendance in classes grew erratic again, would wait for her on the school steps until five, to walk her home, holding hands and strolling by the shop windows, the movie theaters (he loved westerns), and the dance halls on Eighteenth and Vine. They didn't dare wander around Twelfth and Paseo, however, nearly a mile away, where many of the best musicians performed in the town's roughest clubs—the so-called buckets of blood.

They skirted an area that Charlie would shortly be haunting, looking for informal lessons, handouts, and jam sessions to test his mettle. There were large rooms for dancing, like Lincoln Hall, where Alonzo Lewis's best students played, mostly for other teenagers. And there were small, crammed, adults-only clubs like the Cherry Blossom, where Lester Young, Ben Webster, and Herschel Evans, the cream of the city's tenors, challenged and bested the king, Coleman Hawkins; the Subway Club, where Jesse Price terminated a drummers' cutting session by playing a seventy-five

Opposite page: Lester Young, 1936.

. . . .

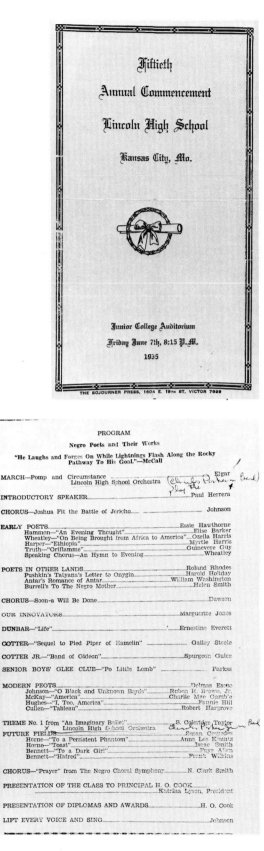

PROGRAM

Negro Poets and Their Works

"He Laughs and Forges On While Lightnings Flash Along the Rocky Pathway To His Goal."—McCall

MARCH—Pomp and Circumstance .... Elgar
    Lincoln High School Orchestra

INTRODUCTORY SPEAKER .... Paul Herrera

CHORUS—Joshua Fit the Battle of Jericho .... Johnson

EARLY POETS .... Essie Hawthorne
  Hammon—"An Evening Thought" .... Elise Barker
  Wheatley—"On Being Brought from Africa to America" ... Ozella Harris
  Harper—"Ethiopia" .... Myrtle Harris
  Truth—"Oriflamme" .... Guinevere Gay
  Speaking Chorus—An Hymn to Evening .... Wheatley

POETS IN OTHER LANDS .... Roland Rhodes
  Pushkin's Tatyana's Letter to Onygin .... Harold Holiday
  Antar's Romance of Antar .... William Washington
  Burrell's To The Negro Mother .... Helen Smith

CHORUS—Soon-a Will Be Done .... Dawson

OUR INNOVATORS .... Marguerite Jones

DUNBAR—"Life" .... Ernestine Everett

COTTER—"Sequel to Pied Piper of Hamelin" .... Gailey Steele

COTTER JR.—"Band of Gideon" .... Spurgeon Guice

SENIOR BOYS' GLEE CLUB—"Po Little Lomb" .... Parkss

MODERN POETS .... Delmas Escoe
  Johnson—"O Black and Unknown Bards" .... Ruben H. Brown, Jr.
  McKay—"America" .... Charlie Mae Camb'e
  Hughes—"I, Too, America" .... Fannie Hill
  Cullen—"Tableau" .... Robert Hargrove

THEME No. 1 from "An Imaginary Ballet" .... S. Coleridge Taylor
  Lincoln High School Orchestra

FUTURE FIELDS .... Susan Cassaden
  Horne—"To a Persistent Phantom" .... Anna Lee Kountz
  Horne—"Toast" .... Isaac Smith
  Bennett—"To a Dark Girl" .... Faye Allen
  Bennett—"Hatred" .... Frank Wilkins

CHORUS—"Prayer" from The Negro Choral Symphony .... N. Clark Smith

PRESENTATION OF THE CLASS TO PRINCIPAL H. O. COOK
  Katrina Lyson, President

PRESENTATION OF DIPLOMAS AND AWARDS .... H. O. Cook

LIFT EVERY VOICE AND SING .... Johnson

The program for Rebecca Ruffin's high school graduation, at which Charlie Parker played baritone horn (with Rebecca's notes).

· · · · · · · · · ·

minute solo on "Nagasaki"; the Sunset, where Pete Johnson played piano and Joe Turner tended bar and sang, his voice carried by an outdoor speaker into the streets; and the Reno Club, a hole-in-the wall where a nine-piece band led by Count Basie and including Lester Young created arrangements out of the air. In those first quiet months of their friendship, Rebecca and Charlie spent their evening on the front-porch swing, and he never spoke about music. She didn't know he was much interested until she saw him playing baritone horn in Lincoln High's marching band the day she graduated. The procession filed by the bandstand and she saw him looking at her as the band played "The Star Spangled Banner." Later they danced, and she was impressed with how sure Charlie was on his feet.

Charlie soon realized that playing baritone horn in the school band was a definite aid in learning harmony. Even more helpful were the older boys who responded to his incessant questions, especially Lawrence Keyes, who lived down the street on Olive. His home was a meeting place for young musicians, and Charlie often practiced there. Keyes played xylophone and cymbals for Alonzo Lewis, but as the leader of the Deans of Swing, he played piano, and he was already in touch with some of the harmonic secrets that puzzled Charlie. "If [Charlie] had been as conscientious about his high school work as he was about his music, he would have become a professor," he later remarked. Parker's obsessive determination didn't guarantee him an easy time, however. He played a ridiculous alto, patched with tinfoil, cellophane, and rubber bands, and he was slow in mastering the rudiments of transposition and improvisation. Incredibly, he knew only one and a half melodies—"Honeysuckle Rose" (he admired Fats Waller) and the first strain of "Lazy River," and a single key (concert F, D on the alto)—when he stopped in at a practice session held by some of the older kids at the Hi-Hat Club and walked right up to the stand. The musicians included saxophonist James Keith and trumpet player James Ross, both of whom later recorded with Harlan Leonard and His Rockets, and a pianist named Shipley Gavan. They immediately went into "Body and Soul," in long meter, and Charlie couldn't find a note. He left fighting back tears, but with the knowledge that he'd have to learn all the keys as well as double-timing.

The acknowledged master of doubling-up (playing at twice the stated tempo) in Kansas City was Buster Smith, an altoist whom many local musicians later recognized as a key influence on Parker. Charlie followed him around and memorized his records. He admired his tart bluesy sound, his rippling phrases, and his rhythmic drive. Yet even while he was teaching himself his craft, mastering each component in his own fashion, he was able to play

professional gigs. Within a year of their first practice session, Keyes had taken him into the Deans of Swing, and Addie went down to the Hurst Loan Shop on Eighteenth and Vine, right near Lincoln Hall where the Deans usually played, and borrowed the money to buy Charlie a used silver-colored Conn in excellent condition. The Deans included James Ross (already a promising arranger as well as a trumpet player), saxophonists Vernon Walker and Freddie Culliver, vocalist Walter Brown (soon to star with McShann's band), and a trombonist named Robert Simpson who many people believe was the closest friend Charlie Parker ever had.

In an interview with Robert Reisner, Keyes spoke of Parker, Simpson, and himself forming a "triumvirate . . . the three of us would hang out in each other's houses, practicing and talking music day and night . . . To say that Charlie admired [Simpson] is perhaps too mild, Charlie worshipped him and was in his company a great deal." Simpson dated Hattie Lee, Mrs. Parker's

The Original Oklahoma City Blue Devils: (left to right) Hot Lips Page, Buster Smith, Thomas Benton, Walter Page, Ermir "Bucket" Coleman (leader until Walter Page took over), Willie Lewis (at piano), Lawrence Williams, Ernie Williams, Thomas Bill Owens, 1928.

. . . .

niece, and seemed to get closer to Charlie than anyone else. When the Deans of Swing broke up, Parker went to work with Oliver Todd at a club called Frankie and Johnny's. The club's owner didn't like Charlie and asked Todd to fire him or pay his salary out of his own pocket. As Todd recalled the incident to Stanley Crouch, Simpson was suffering from pneumonia and a heart ailment, yet he took a streetcar to the club to beg Todd not to fire him. Simpson argued that Charlie had an inferiority complex and needed encouragement; he predicted Charlie would attain greatness as a musician. A few days later Simpson died at twenty-one on the operating table from what Keyes had heard was a heart ailment. Charlie was inconsolable, and the tragedy may have contributed to his sudden appetite for benzedrine inhalers, pot, and liquor. Shortly before his death, Parker would tell Ahmed Basheer (as quoted by Reisner), "I don't let anyone get too close to me, even you." Asked why, he answered, "Once in Kansas City I had a friend who I liked very much, and a sorrowful thing happened. . . . He died."

During the year and a half that Charlie played with Keyes, they usually worked weekend dances at Lincoln Hall, which had overflowing crowds of young people. As a nonunion band, it worked for a percentage of the door (admission was a quarter), and on a good night each man might take home ten to fifteen dollars. He was heard with other bands as well, though he didn't impress anyone other than Simpson. Indeed, he had another humiliation in store, probably in the spring of 1936. On that night, Count Basie finished the late set at the Reno Club, and a jam session was organized with the imperial Jo Jones presiding at the drums. Charlie had taken to hanging around the notoriously rowdy club to hear Lester Young; the room had a balcony in which he could sit undisturbed and soak up the kinds of lessons that had the most value for him. "The actual experience, to be around the thing in person, is what counts," Jones once told Stanley Dance. As an example he mentioned the glory years in Kansas City, where there were "farm teams. You played down here and then you graduated. It was like going from grade school, to high school, to college. You didn't just jump into a particular thing until you were ready." Charlie decided to jump during Jones's jam session, and after he played a couple of faltering choruses at a racing tempo, Jones hit his bell in imitation of Major Bowes. Charlie didn't take the hint. After a couple of additional unheeded gongs, Jones lifted his cymbal off its stand and sent it crashing at Parker's feet. The altoist left amid cruel laughter, vowing to return and show them up.

Meanwhile, his courting of Rebecca proceeded as quickly as his music. For two years, they had strolled through Kansas City, hand

in hand, attending movies and sharing popcorn and cherry sodas. That ended when one of Rebecca's sisters caught them in his room and promptly reported the news to Fannie Ruffin, a strict Methodist who would whip her children for improprieties. She decided the family would have to move. Rebecca was ordered not to see Charlie, but another of her sisters helped her to sneak out for their continued rendezvous, which, she points out, were entirely innocent. Her beau was still quite the proper young man. When told of the statement he made years later about dissipating at twelve and using heroin at fifteen, Rebecca exclaimed, "Charlie's crazy!" We had to take tests in school to check for pregnancies and venereal disease. If he had been using drugs then, it would have showed up on the tests." She insists that he began using narcotics in 1937, which confirms the recollections of other friends and musicians in Kansas City. By that time, she had become Charlie's bride. On a Friday evening, three months after the Ruffins moved out, Charlie and Rebecca were sitting on the steps of Crispus Attucks and he proposed. She went home, packed, in-

Various Kansas City nightclubs: (left to right, top to bottom) Dante's Inferno, 512 East 12th Street, a white club showcasing female impersonators; Harlem Nightclub, 1414 East 15th Street, where Benny Moten's band played; Red and Dutch; Wiggle Inn, 2607 Troost Street; Hey-Hay Club, 4th and Cherry Streets, where Charlie Parker played with George E. Lee; unknown; Deluxe Nightclub; King Kong Lair, 520 East 12th Street, where white bands played, 1937.

formed her mother of her decision, and moved back to Olive Street.

Addie took the news with her customary stoical efficiency and proceeded to superintend all the details. She asked Charlie to stay out that night after work with the Keyes band, so that she could help Rebecca fashion a wedding dress. The next day, July 25, 1936, they went to the courthouse, and Rebecca, dressed in yellow and white, and holding a white Bible Addie had bought her, became Mrs. Charlie Parker. When the justice of the peace asked Charlie for the ring, he didn't have one. Addie removed the rings his father had given to her and gave them to Charlie. She also signed the certificate of marriage since bride and groom were both sixteen. On returning home, they were greeted by Charlie Sr., whom Rebecca had never previously seen, and his brother and Ikey and some other relatives, as well as Hattie Lee and Marie Goldin, the two boarders who moved in after the Ruffins left. Addie served cake, ice cream, and punch. A naive Rebecca locked her door that night but eventually gave way to her husband's entreaties.

She had several surprises in store for herself during the next couple of years. Shortly after they married, Charlie tore or infected his foreskin and disappeared for two weeks, during which time Addie would tell her only that he'd gone for a cure. Many years later, she learned that he had gone to Wheatley, Kansas, where Dr. J. R. Thompson, who had delivered him, performed a circumcision. Parker was impotent during the period of healing and was so ashamed that for several weeks he refused to talk to Rebecca, who was afraid to press the issue with him or Addie. He announced his return to health with an astonishing, unprecedented blast of music. One afternoon she was lying down upstairs when she heard him playing the Conn alto. She ran downstairs to find him "blowing his brains out" for about seven minutes, eyes shut, deep in concentration, impassioned and resolute. She asked: Why did he play so long, why didn't he relax? But he opened his eyes and merely smiled, then sat down at the piano and played a variation on Fats Waller's "Stealin' Apples," which he dedicated to her. She noticed the spur to his imagination still in place on the victrola: Fletcher Henderson's version of Waller's tune, featuring Roy Eldridge and Leon "Chu" Berry. Parker had seen Berry, one of the most highly admired tenor saxophonists in the country, during his visit to a local club, and was enthralled by him. Charlie's explosion of sustained playing was the first indication she had of the progress he'd made.

November brought another surprise. During the preceding months, Charlie had taken to spending almost all of his time downstairs practicing. Since he stayed out late, and sometimes all

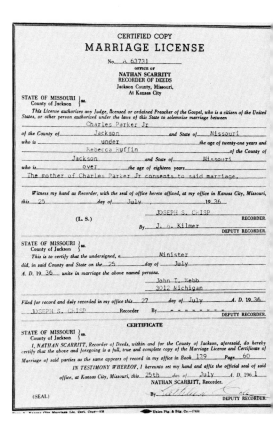

Rebecca Ruffin and Charlie Parker's marriage license, July 25, 1936, Kansas City, Missouri.

Lester Young, Ed Lewis, Count Basie, Jo Jones, at the Apollo Theatre, New York City, 1940.

night, Rebecca didn't see him much. She never went to the clubs. In order to study beyond the gaze of Kansas City's disapproving eyes, Charlie began working in Jefferson City in the Ozarks with Ernie Daniels. On Thanksgiving, he embarked on the 150-mile trip in a Chevrolet with Daniels and the band's bassist, George Wilkerson. The car, speeding to its destination, skidded on a sheet of ice and overturned more than once before crashing off the road. Daniels was hospitalized for a month with a punctured lung, and Wilkerson was killed, staked by a peg from his bass. Charlie was lucky. He broke three ribs and fractured his spine, but he didn't require hospitalization. He returned to the Parker home trussed in bandages, much to the horror of Rebecca and Addie, who hadn't heard about the accident. Although the silver Conn was destroyed in the car, money from a lawsuit enabled him to buy his first Selmer, a gold saxophone that he would pawn countless times but which remained his preferred brand until 1947, when he switched to King for his sessions with strings. He didn't get to work out on the Selmer right away, of course. For two months, he lay upstairs recuperating, his pillow filled with a stash of marijuana—which was still legal—and his needs attended to by four doting women: Rebecca, Addie, Hattie Lee, and Marie. "The women in that house loved Charlie," Rebecca says. "Except Parky—she worshipped him."

When Charlie was healed, he lied about his age and joined the union, largely through the good offices of George E. Lee, a popular Kansas City bandleader who occasionally fronted the Keyes band as a singer. In a few weeks, he was taking weekly gigs in Eldon, Missouri, in the Ozarks, with Tommy Douglas's septet. In some ways, he seemed renewed, less aloof, more given to joking, especially when he fooled around with benzedrine capsules, which he would break, soak in wine or cola, and inhale. He amused the guys in the band by imitating the basso growl of Popeye with his voice and on his alto, and he began to display the ability, widely noted in his New York years, to discourse with learned authority on any subject. He also displayed the unpredictable behavior that would mar the rest of his career, staying up all night and sleeping through jobs. He looked shabby, threadbare. The other musicians sometimes took custody of his band jacket so it would be presentable for the gig.

Around this time Mary Lou Williams heard him play with Andy Kirk's wife, Mary Kirk, a pianist who favored a formal quasi-rag style and an oom-pah bass. To Williams, Charlie played "just the way he did when he was in New York and it sounded funny." That is surely an exaggeration. Yet Parker's playing was different enough from the prevailing style not only to elicit comments concerning his imcompatibility with Kirk, but to impress the newly arrived Oklahoman, Jay McShann, who told him first time out, "You don't play like anybody else in Kansas City." Indeed, McShann remains incredulous about the fiasco at the Reno Club: "I've heard more tales about when he wasn't playing. He was playing good the first time I heard him. If that story about Jo Jones throwing a cymbal happened, it happened before 1937." Evidence to support McShann's impression recently surfaced in the form of an amateur disc-recording made by Clarence Davis, a member of Tommy Douglas's band. Davis recorded several unaccompanied Parker solos, but only one has survived: it's a three-and-a-half-minute medley of "Honeysuckle Rose," the first tune Parker taught himself, and "Body and Soul," the cause of his first jam-session downfall. Although the disc has been framed by its present owner with the legend "1937," it was probably recorded a year or two later—Davis isn't certain. Nonetheless, it represents Parker's first recording, and it shows him wrestling with an

Mary Lou Williams with Remo Palmier, New York City, 1947.

acidic tone, double-time, triplets, and rococo embellishments. The latter, in union with a soft-beat/hard-beat rhythmic gait, suggests the influence of Hawkins and Chu Berry. Occasional incoherence—especially at the eight-bar transitional passages (musicians call them turnbacks)—and an overall lack of poise underscore the youthfulness of the performance.

Because of his weekly trips to Eldon with Tommy Douglas, a virtuoso saxophonist and clarinetist, Charlie was always in the company of older musicians, and his willingness to be influenced by them took an unexpected direction. Some of the guys were raising families. Charlie decided he wanted a child, too—a son. When the mechanics of conception didn't proceed as quickly as he expected, he consulted his mother, who provided him with a tonic. Rebecca was pregnant by spring. At first Charlie was elated, but then the Eldon job ended and he hit the streets in search of work, finding only one-nighters. His moods were erratic, his manner distant. Strange visitors were tramping up and down the stairs of the Parker home. In July, Rebecca got her first look at a needle. She was three months pregnant when Charlie called her upstairs and told her to sit on the bed. He was wearing a dark suit and a long tie. It was night and the shade was down. She looked toward the window where a small mirror was set and saw in its reflection the tie pulled tight around his arm, the needle plunging in and the blood coming up. She screamed, "What are you doing?" He just looked and smiled. He wiped the blood, and slipped the tie off his arm and around his neck, and said, "Well, I'll be seeing you, Rebec." He kissed her on the forehead and left. Rebecca looked in the drawer and found his setup. She took it down and showed it to Addie, who didn't say a word. Next morning, Addie told him, "Charlie, I'd rather see you dead than use that stuff." He glowered at Rebecca and disappeared for two weeks.

By summer he was back in Eldon with the ubiquitous George E. Lee, who for more than a decade had led the band at Kansas City's Lyric Hall. Now he was in charge of a small group at a resort spot in the Ozarks, Lake Taneycomo, with rhythm guitarist Efferge Ware and pianist Carrie Powell, both of whom furthered Charlie's education with instruction in harmony. Ware was particularly supportive, pragmatic as well as discerning. He not only showed him the cycle of fifths and the value of passing chords, but encouraged him to sit in at the Subway Club, where he often worked. Additional lessons were available through records. Count Basie, who was born in New Jersey and got stranded in Kansas City, made it back East in style. His debut session with a quintet had just been released, and it featured radiantly melodic solos by Lester Young. In a few days, Charlie knew those solos by heart.

Without formal training, Charlie adhered to the golden rule of

Opposite page: Charlie Parker, Pleyel, Paris, 1949.

· · · · · · · · · ·

4 6

the autodidact: if it sounds good, it is good. Immersed in the ceremony of mastering an art for which there are complicated techniques but no absolute procedures, he worked feverishly to soak up workshop secrets and traditions. Despite occasional assertions of self, he moved cautiously through the Kansas City jazz world, preparing himself not for the moment when it would offer him acceptance, but when he could supersede local ritual and, fueled by everything he'd learned, take flight. Like any good apprentice, he sought worthy masters and accommodated their teachings in grateful humility. Buster "Prof" Smith contracted a large band at the Reno that fall, with Jesse Price and McShann. He hired Charlie as second alto and took him under his wing, advising him on how to shave thick reeds in order to project a bold, bright sound. Charlie never missed a rehearsal, never even showed up late. He called Smith Dad and often visited his house for extra sessions. When the band went into the Antlers, Parker openly emulated the older man's improvisations.

Weeks later McShann managed to get a booking for his own group at a place called Martin's, and he used the young altoist, too. But when that job ended, Charlie was on the streets again, taking whatever work he could. In less than three years, he had metamorphosed from a bright, ingenuous kid—partial to the usual

Probably Eddie Nicholson, Bill DeArango, unknown, Ben Webster, Charlie Parker, at the Onyx, New York City, 1943.

childish diversions, indifferently fond of music—to a disheveled musician, convinced of his own destiny, yet reckless with the appetites that could only undermine his future. Once considered boyish, he was now thought older than his years by virtually everyone who knew him. As he rid himself of baby fat and grew to his full height of nearly five feet eleven inches, he carried himself with increasing authority, and developed a knack for leading several lives. An expert mimic and a fast wit, he could disarm even those who knew he'd end up "borrowing" the shirts off their backs. He had presence, a ready smile, a shy flirtatious gleam in the eyes. Is it possible that no one was merely indifferent to him? Those who didn't love him hated him. (Dave Dexter, Jr., a record producer, spoke for the dissenters in a vicious ad hominem attack, published in 1964. Yet even he finished on the usual note of awe: "There will never be another like him.") Most of those who knew him bear witness to Charlie's spunky charm. They feel he had a right to the uncommon attention and forbearance he demanded of everyone who loved him.

Buster Smith.

The severest trials were suffered at home. Charlie began to look haggard, rumpled. Pockets formed beneath his eyes. He acted with supreme indifference to the problems of the women with whom he lived, sometimes lashing out in violence. The drug traffic continued. Addie's curse had had no effect. Charlie ignored Rebecca, brushing by her without so much as a hello. Once he asked her to get an abortion. When she refused, the subject was dropped. Things disappeared from the house: an iron, jewelry, a radio, clothing. He was pawning everything he could get his hands on, and Rebecca made a point of hiding her churchgoing dress. He took up with another woman, whose identity Rebecca discovered when he left a couple of letters under a pillow. She read them and put them back. Yet they weren't there when he looked for them the next day. He called her upstairs and told her to sit on the bed and look out the window. She heard a click. Charlie was holding a gun to her temple and demanding the letters. She told him to look in his bureau where he usually put mail, and there they were. As he descended the steps, Rebecca threw a flatiron at him, which crashed through the glass panes near the front door. Mrs. Parker walked to the banister and asked, "What is it, dearie?"

Then his mood reversed. He returned broke and despondent, looking desperate, when Rebecca was in her sixth month. At times he acted like his old self. On the night Marie and Rebecca went to Lincoln Hall to see Charlie play, he danced with her, big stomach and all. When she delivered on January 10, 1938, he was away on a gig, but before leaving he asked her please not to name the baby in his absence. "Just call it Baby Parker," he said. He

. . . .

wanted to name his son himself. Nearly a week later, he did: Francis Leon, after Francis Scott Key, whose "The Star Spangled Banner" was the first piece Rebecca had heard him play, and Leon "Chu" Berry. The presence of the infant, known by his middle name, did little to alleviate the problems between Charlie and Rebecca, whose marriage was now tolerable at best.

Charlie was usually away from home. He'd taken a gig at a place in the suburbs, about thirty minutes outside of town, owned by Tutty Clarkin, a brash eccentric who liked to be surrounded by animals, including a goat named T. J. Pendergast and a parrot that squawked "nigger." Tutty's Mayfair catered to a white middle-class audience and charged good money; the musicians earned about fifteen dollars each per week. The group, consisting of five pieces and a woman singer, played for dancing and listening. They depended on Charlie's arrangements, which inconvenienced Clarkin, who was habitually impatient with Parker and would have fired him if the other musicians hadn't intervened. The nights of wandering around the district, soaking up Ellington (he loved his harmonic palette and the swirling solos by Barney Bigard) and Basie, of sitting in movie theaters concentrating on the scores, had paid off. Charlie had become a distinctive writer, experimenting with flatted fifths and augmented thirteenths. His favorite tune was Ray Noble's "Cherokee," which he was constantly rearranging. One week he brought in a new version every night, including one with a 138-measure intro. He also worked on improving his thin sound, especially after he acquired a new horn. In a rage one night, he battered the recalcitrant alto he was playing against the curb. Clarkin would later recall to Reisner that he magnanimously bought Charlie a new Selmer. Winston Williams, the group's bassist, told Crouch that Clarkin put up the money reluctantly, after Williams convinced him of the necessity and agreed to stand surety for it.

The party was over in Tom's Town. While Pendergast awaited trial on a tax-fraud charge, the city fathers proceeded to close many of the clubs. Buster Smith took an offer from Basie to help him with arrangements at the Famous Door in New York, where the band was doing big business. McShann hoped to use Charlie again, but now he was touring with a group in Chicago. Some of the guys were playing in Swope Park. There was no place else to go. To make matters worse, Charlie got involved in an altercation with a cab driver over a ten-dollar tab he couldn't pay. The driver tried to snatch his horn and Charlie nicked him with a knife. He spent some time—accounts range from overnight to three weeks—in jail. When he got out, he wanted out of Kansas City. He pawned his alto, strolled to the outskirts of town, and stole a ride on a freight train fleeing to Chicago.

Opposite page: Leon "Chu" Berry, 1938.

. . . .

5 0 🎵

3

APPRENTICESHIP

WHEN CHARLIE LANDED in Chicago, most likely in the fall of 1938, before the bitter winds — the Chicago hawk — hit, he was as thin as the rails that had brought him and not much better for wear. Bedraggled and exhausted, he nonetheless made his way in the early morning hours to the 65 Club, near Michigan Avenue and Fifty-fifth Street, where a breakfast dance was in progress. The featured band, a quintet led by King Kolax, was on a break, and a few of the guys were on the street smoking with some friends, including Billy Eckstine and Budd Johnson. Charlie— "the raggedest guy you'd want to see," as Eckstine described him to Reisner—walked over to bum a cigarette but otherwise held back. Later, inside, he asked the band's alto saxophonist, Goon Gardner, if he could play his horn. In Eckstine's words, "This cat gets up there, and I'm telling you he blew the hell off that thing!" Everyone turned to listen, including Johnson, who was mesmerized: "I couldn't believe it. I said, 'What!'" Afterward, Parker went to the bar and introduced himself to Johnson, telling how he used to play stickball in front of George E. Lee's mother's house in K.C. when Budd and the others rehearsed, and how he would peep through the window and listen. Gardner took him home, gave him some clothes and a clarinet, and got him a few jobs. Within weeks the clarinet was in the pawnshop and Charlie was on a bus headed for New York.

Charlie wasted no time in locating his mentor. He turned up on Buster Smith's doorstep, frayed and hungry, legs swollen from having worn his shoes so long. Smith and his wife put him up, allowing him to use their bed by day, since he was out all night hanging around clubs, listening to music and looking for work. That first night he walked over to the Savoy Ballroom and stood outside, staring at the marquee, marveling at the fact that he was in New York, and dreaming of the day he'd play on its most famous bandstand. But jobs were scarce even for locals, with so

Opposite page: Charlie Parker, Los Angeles, 1946.

many good players on the scene. For a transient without a union card, they hardly existed. When the Smiths lost patience, he took his only nonmusical job, scrubbing dishes at a popular Harlem hangout called Jimmy's Chicken Shack. His hours were midnight to eight and his pay nine dollars a week. The one compensation was the featured performer, Art Tatum. Blind, rotund, and regal of manner, Tatum was an astonishing pianist, unequaled in his harmonic ingenuity or his ability to execute abrupt tempo changes and rapid-fire modulations. His pristine embellishments were packaged in glittery arpeggios and topped with wittily juxtaposed melodic figures (often quotations from pop songs). Virtually all the key jazz modernists name Tatum as a major influence, but none received so concentrated a course from him as the diffident dishwasher at Jimmy's, who was too shy to say hello yet continued in a disagreeable job for the entire three months of Tatum's engagement.

Eventually Charlie found a few musical or semimusical gigs. He even played at a Times Square tango palace. But he also sat in—for free or a meal or cigarette money—at Clark Monroe's Uptown House on 138th Street, where some of the more adventurous musicians in town came to jam, though no one seems to have paid him much mind. He made friends with a guitarist named Bill "Biddy" Fleet, who rivaled Buster Smith as a valuable sounding board for Charlie's constant questions about harmonic theory. Perhaps the most important idea Parker learned from observing Tatum was that any note could be made to fit in a chord if it was suitably resolved. With Fleet, he pursued that notion, practicing passing tones and concentrating on the higher intervals of chords—raised ninths, elevenths, thirteenths. His obsession helped to buffer him from the indifference and downright scorn of other musicians, who thought he played funny or wrong. Yet despite his difficulty in finding work or acceptance, he was choosy about the musicians with whom he played and practiced. He was perfecting a music that would eventually send his detractors running for cover. Virtuosity is the best revenge.

Although most musicians concentrated on a few select keys, easy chord progressions, and moderate tempos, Parker persistently raised difficult problems and sought complicated solutions. He reveled in songs with challenging chord changes like "All God's Chillun Got Rhythm"; "Get Happy"; and especially his personal showpiece, "Cherokee," a pop song that was nonetheless a jam session terror because of the fast-moving harmony in its middle section. Fleet and Parker often began the evening by practicing in the back room at Dan Wall's Chili House, down the street from Monroe's, and it was there that the great epiphany occurred:

Art Tatum, c. 1949.

Charlie Parker: three stills from a film directed by
Gjon Mili but never released because the soundtrack
was lost, c. 1951.

· · · · · · · · · · · · ·

5 5

I remember one night before Monroe's I was jamming in a chili house on Seventh Avenue between 139th and 140th. It was December 1939. Now I'd been getting bored with the stereotyped changes that were being used at the time, and I kept thinking there's bound to be something else. I could hear it sometimes but I couldn't play it. Well, that night I was working over "Cherokee," and as I did I found that by using the higher intervals of a chord as a melody line and backing them with appropriately related changes, I could play the thing I'd been hearing. I came alive.

Parker had liberated himself from the obvious melody notes, or the lower intervals implied in any set of chord changes. He found that the more subtle upper intervals, which tended toward dissonance, could be tamed through resolutions that would make them consistent with the underlying harmonic contour. He had flown the coop from cliché, but not from the rigors of making a living in a conventional world. He took a job with a small show band led by one Banjo Burney, which drove down to Maryland for three weeks. There he received a telegram and a train ticket from

Jay McShann, 1938.

. . . .

5 6

Addie. His father was dead, stabbed by a jealous woman—some say a prostitute. He went home for the funeral.

Almost as soon as he was situated in Kansas City again, he was hired by Harlan Leonard, an officious taskmaster whose band included several of Charlie's friends and acquaintances—James Ross, James Keith, Jesse Price, Winston Williams—as well as a brilliant new arranger and pianist from Cleveland, Tadd Dameron. Charlie and Tadd became friends right off, having at least two interests in common. First, Tadd was as harmonically adventurous as Charlie and knew more theory. Once while practicing "Lady Be Good," Charlie was so taken with the pianist's substitute chords that he put down his alto, ran over, and kissed him. Second, Tadd could do all sorts of tricks with pharmaceuticals and had a big appetite for getting high. About the only person in the Rockets who didn't get along with Charlie was the leader, who had the makings of an excellent band and an unfortunate habit of counting off tempos too fast for the music (that responsibility was soon given to Jimmy Keith). He entrusted Charlie with several solos, including "Cherokee," but couldn't abide his frequent lateness. After four or five weeks, he fired him.

Which was a break for Jay McShann, who now had a big band of his own and was getting ready to go on the road. McShann's was the band of choice for many of the younger players, and it may be that Charlie forced Leonard's hand. (Dameron also admired McShann and wrote arrangements for him on the sly.) . . . .

(Left to right) Buddy Anderson, Bob Mabane, Gus Johnson, Orville "Piggy" Minor, Charlie Parker, Gene Ramey, Jay McShann, Wichita, Kansas, December 2, 1940.

During a Battle of the Bands between Leonard and McShann, Charlie asked Jay if he could go with him and was advised to give two weeks' notice. Perhaps Charlie couldn't wait the two weeks and behaved accordingly. In any case, they were together again, and Charlie was delighted. Rebecca, with whom he was briefly reconciled, noted an improvement in his mood during this period. She became pregnant again, but complications set in and she miscarried in July. During a visit to the hospital, as Charlie waited in the lobby, Rebecca asked Dr. Thompson about the needles her husband used. Thompson told her that if he continued, he'd never see forty; he gave him, at best, another eighteen to twenty years. Still, Addie refused to interfere, and Rebecca gave up mentioning the subject. She and Charlie no longer argued. Whatever he wanted, she acquiesced. They were marking time. Later that year, Charlie asked for a divorce. He told her, "If I were free, Rebec, I think I could become a great musician." He had already asked Addie to allow Rebecca and Leon to continue living in the house.

Rebecca remembers Duke Ellington coming through town and trying to recruit Charlie, who demurred, claiming he wasn't up to the regimen of rehearsals and one-nighters. Yet he was ready to travel with the McShann orchestra, the last great territory band. Here was his conduit to recognition, as well as a nickname that stuck for the rest of his life and after. En route to a school date at the University of Nebraska, the car Charlie was in hit a couple of farm chickens that ran onto the road. According to McShann, Charlie told the driver, "Man, go back, you hit that yardbird." They turned around, and when they got to where the dead chicken lay, Charlie jumped out and returned with it cradled in his arms. Upon arriving in Lincoln, he asked the lady of the house where they boarded if she would cook it for dinner. She complied, much to the amusement of the other musicians, who began calling Charlie "Yardbird" or "Yard" or "Bird." By the time he resurfaced in New York, he was generally known as Bird, which is how he often referred to himself. For the next three and a half years, he had a semipermanent home in McShann's band. At Jay's urging, he took occasional leaves of absence when the drugs had the best of him and he couldn't "make time." As McShann puts it, "Bird got to moving pretty fast and every once in a while we'd tell him, 'Why don't you cool down and rest yourself up for a week?' So he'd say, 'OK, Hootie [McShann's nickname],' and a week later he'd come back and join the band."

Yet when he was feeling good, he was McShann's right-hand man. He rehearsed the reed section, played many solos, and kept everyone in good spirits with his jokes, wisecracks, general playfulness, and immense capacity for eating—two full dinners at a

Opposite page: Charlie Parker, unknown, Duke Ellington, c. 1950.

. . . .

(Left to right) Jay McShann, Leonard Enois, Gene Ramey, Gus Johnson, Bob Mabane, Charlie Parker, Buddy Anderson, Bob Merrill, John Jackson, Orville Minor, Freddie Culiver, Lawrence Anderson, Joe Baird, at the Savoy Ballroom, New York City, 1941.

sitting was not unusual. One night he got the reed players high on huge quantities of nutmeg, and when McShann cued their entrance, they simply fell out laughing. Yet as an example of his thoroughness as a musician, McShann tells of his rivalry with the band's expert lead altoist:

> We had a young cat called John Jackson—J.J., they called him. And Bird came to me once and told me, "Man, this cat is just reading circles around me." He says, "I tell you what. I won't make rehearsals for the next couple of days, because I'd rather go in the woodshed on this cat cause he's making me look bad. But I'll tell you what you do. When you play the date Friday night, if I miss a note you can fine me." So sure enough, we'd been rehearsing on this stuff that Bird hadn't seen. But Bird played it that night better than the cats that'd been rehearsing.

McShann was solidly in Bird's corner and it disturbed him that audiences couldn't comprehend what he was playing. The farther they traveled from the Southwest, the less response his solos received. To his colleagues, however, Bird was another reason for living.

Parker was achieving the kind of fluency that only the greats can claim: complete authority from the first lick, and the ability to sustain the initial inspiration throughout a solo, so that it has dramatic coherence. His tone became increasingly sure, waxing in volume despite the deliberate lack of vibrato. It was candid and unswerving, and it had a cold blues edge unlike that of any of his predecessors. The musicians in New York had tried to intimidate him into aping the clean, pear-shaped sound of Benny Carter or the rhapsodic richness of Johnny Hodges. His contemporaries in McShann's band knew what he was after. They were amused, too, by how fast his mind worked, as he imitated sounds echoing in from the street—engines, backfiring tires, auto horns—and worked them into musical phrases. He not only mastered Tatum's trick of juxtaposing discursive melodies in such a way that they fit right into the harmonic structure of the song he was playing, but took it another step: he quoted melodies that had lyrical relevance to the moment. He might nod to a woman in blue with a snippet of "Alice Blue Gown," or to a woman in red with "The Lady in Red," or comment on a woman headed for the ladies' room with "I Know Where You're Going." He had a ripe eye for women.

When the band reached Wichita, it was recorded for the first time: broadcast transcriptions for station KFBI. Never intended for commercial release, they remained unknown outside a cabal of Parker collectors until 1974. To contemporary ears, Parker's solos sound like an exercise in autobiography, replete with bows to those who influenced him as well as intimations of things to come. "Body and Soul" follows the format of the Chu Berry-Roy Eldridge record, but in the second eight bars of his solo, Parker cites a passage from Coleman Hawkins's version. With "Lady Be Good," he pays hearty tribute to Lester Young, even as he undermines Young's lyricism with his acidic timbre. On "Moten Swing," however, he attempts a rococo conceit à la Chu and loses his footing in the second eight bars. The background riff on "Wichita Blues" is a piece he later recorded as "The Hymn." Best of all is his fleet variation on his old friend, "Honeysuckle Rose," which unfolds as a burst of melodic reverie, each turnback navigated with graceful aplomb.

The band was now on its way. It boasted an elegantly aggressive rhythm section in McShann's bluesy, Hines-inspired piano, Gene Ramey's bass, and Gus Johnson's drums, and a powerful ensemble including John Jackson's mighty lead alto and two good trumpet soloists. For singers, it had two unknowns who became jukebox favorites. McShann first heard Walter Brown, who sang blues, on his arrival in Kansas City. After Brown's set, Jay had followed him off the stand and paid him his last fifty cents to reprise a blues he'd sung. He recruited ballad singer Al Hibbler in San Antonio, after the blind baritone crooner pestered him into

Dizzy Gillespie, c. 1945.

letting him sit in. Above all, the band had something genuinely new to offer: Charlie Parker. When Dizzy Gillespie came through Kansas City with Cab Calloway's band, McShann's trumpet soloists, Orville Minor and Buddy Anderson, went to see him and were so impressed with Gillespie's new ideas that they invited him to the musician's local to jam with Bird. They showed their man off like a prize marlin.

By spring, McShann had an efficient management company behind him and a long tour mapped out that would bring them eastward into the deep South, where they would sample a kind of racism far more virulent than anything in Missouri. When their train pulled into that station in Jackson, Mississippi, the first thing they saw was a man walking with a ball and chain—a harbinger, as it turned out. One night Parker and Walter Brown were arrested for sitting on the porch of a boardinghouse with a light burning after "curfew." After a couple of nights in jail, Bird memorialized the incident in a song he called "What Price Love." In later years, he taught the lyric to Carmen McRae, Earl Coleman (who recorded it with Fats Navarro), and others, but it never caught on. The music, however, became instantly famous when he recorded it in 1946, as "Yardbird Suite."

As the band prepared to pull out of New Orleans, McShann learned that Decca Records was willing to record the band, now enlarged to eleven pieces, in Dallas. They turned west again and arrived in the studio on April 30, 1941. On the superb Willie Scott arrangement of "Swingmatism," McShann gives the last two bars of his piano solo to Parker as a pickup, and Bird uses it to launch a flowing invention. "Hootie Blues" proffers not only a Parker blues chorus (with a characteristic riff figure) that perked the interest of many young musicians around the country, but also shows off his wit as an arranger. Behind the opening theme, Bird had the ensemble play "Donkey Serenade," which had recently been recorded by Artie Shaw (whose playing was admired by Parker and Buster Smith). Parker did not appear on the number that ultimately guaranteed the band a ticket to New York. "Confessin' the Blues" was performed by just the rhythm section and Walter Brown, and it became a runaway rhythm-and-blues hit, selling more than a half-million copies. The band faced east again: Chicago (more recordings), Detroit, and finally the Savoy Ballroom in New York.

The McShann band descended on New York in a caravan of three cars and a truck that held the instruments and the music. Bird drove in the truck and took over the wheel as they neared the city. On a whim, he decided on the scenic route and crossed illegally into Central Park. When a mounted cop stopped him, he went into his lost-rube routine, complete with stutter, and was

· · · · · · · · · ·

told to get the hell out of there. They stayed at the Woodside Hotel, along with several other bands, and were greeted by Kansas
City veterans who'd beat them to the Apple. That night at the Savoy, billed opposite Lucky Millinder, whose band included Gillespie and Sister Rosetta Tharpe, McShann triumphed. As did
Parker, at least as far as the cognoscenti were concerned. He was
featured in two blazing show-stoppers, "Cherokee" and "Clap
Hands, Here Comes Charlie." Ben Webster ran downtown and
told the musicians on Fifty-second Street to get up to the Savoy to
take some lessons. Many came and admired, including Jimmy
Dorsey, a pioneering pop altoist with impeccable technique who
had inspired several jazz players to choose the instrument. He is
said to have given Parker a few hundred dollars to buy a new alto.

Many others, however, were put off by Parker's visionary talent.
Their reluctance to acknowledge his achievement greatly disturbed McShann, who recognized Bird as primarily a blues
player—"the greatest blues player in the world." His disappoint-
ment in ungenerous musicians was underscored by the indifference of the audience, which preferred the rumbling, honking solos
of tenor saxophonist Jimmy Forrest (who was hired on Bird's ad-

Jam session at the Heatwave, New York City, 1944:
(left to right) Eddie Dougherty, Jimmy Phipps, Hot
Lips Page, Allen Tinney, Don Byas, Herbert Francis
Jenkins (behind Byas), David Van Dyke, Dud
Bascomb, Buck Jones (playing bass), Charlie Parker,
Bill Spooner (standing in rear), Art Phipps, unknown
trombone, Johnny Hicks.

vice): "It used to bug me that it took so long for people to find out what was happening. Bird would get through blowing everything there is to blow, and the people never clapped, never moved, nothing. But when Jimmy Forrest started, he'd tear the house up. People went crazy." The huge swing audience never completely grasped Parker's music, but through broadcasts emanating from the Savoy, most musicians quickly came around, as did a new generation of fans. Parker's countless choruses on "Cherokee" were a call to arms for young players who'd been exploring similarly advanced ideas in improvisation. His technique and speed, logic and lyricism, fire and shrewdness all added up to a way out of the woodshed of experimentation and into the light of accomplishment.

Although he appeared with McShann fitfully for nearly four years, there were few records: only one session in New York, on July 2, 1942. Parker's solo on "Sepian Bounce," a Jimmie Lunceford-influenced arrangement with a prescient brass flourish before the piano solo, is sure but rhythmically cool, exhibiting little of the volatility to come. (In his *Down Beat* Blindfold Test in 1948, Parker dismissed it as "dated, antiquated.") On "The Jumpin' Blues," his chorus opens with a phrase that was later expanded by Little Benny Harris into a modernist anthem, "Ornithology" (based not on the blues, but on the song "How High the Moon"). Those solos scarcely capture the excitement Parker is said to have

Charlie Parker at the Royal Roost, New York City, 1949.

generated on the band's radio broadcasts. Nor does a privately re-corded version of "Cherokee," made that year at Monroe's; his performance is incandescent in parts, but his phrasing of the re-lease is uncharacteristically contrived. The chance to record in a studio was squelched indefinitely when James Petrillo, the des-potic head of the American Federation of Musicians, instigated a recording ban to settle the issue of a musicians' trust fund.

The strike lasted two years. As a result, the genesis of modern jazz—bebop, as it would popularly be known—was shrouded in an uncommon secrecy. Only the musicians themselves were privy to the making of a new musical movement, and for a couple of years their labors bore fruit chiefly in the confines of after-hours jam sessions. Parker was now received with a great deal more respect than when he first appeared in New York. Not yet twenty-two, he was a focal point at the dazzling contests at Monroe's, where young musicians and established ones dropped by to hear him and, if they had enough courage, share the stage. At Minton's Playhouse, originally the dining area of the neighboring Hotel Cecil, a new music policy had been introduced in 1939 by Teddy Hill, the erstwhile bandleader who once employed such incipient modernists as Dizzy Gillespie and Kenny Clarke. He chose Clarke and pianist Thelonious Monk to lead a house band for jam ses-

Thelonious Monk, Howard McGhee, Roy Eldridge, Teddy Hill, at Minton's Playhouse, New York City, 1947.

sions on Monday nights and succeeded in attracting distinguished as well as aspiring musicians. Held in cheerful violation of prohibitive union rules, those sessions were a training ground for the new music. Clarke, Monk, Gillespie, and others shared and elaborated their musical discoveries, often conspiring to scare musicians outside the clique by inserting passing chords, or stomping off hair-raisingly fast tempos.

In Gillespie's autobiography, bassist Milt Hinton tells how he and Dizzy would go to the roof during intermissions at the Cotton Club, where they appeared with Cab Calloway's orchestra, and prepare gambits for Minton's. Gillespie would tell him, "Now look, when we go down to the jam session, we're gonna say we're gonna play, 'I Got Rhythm,' but we're gonna use these changes." He would then run down a complicated sequence of chords. At Minton's, the hopeful players were "left right at the post . . . eventually they would put their horns away, and we could go on and blow in peace and get our little exercise." Needless to say, resentments swelled. The young Turks were serving notice that the old formulas were no longer good enough. They were in rebellion not only against the banalization of "our music" by commercial interests, but against the morass of clichés that governed so many improvisations. What they offered was not simply an elevated harmonic intricacy, but a new articulation.

It is now commonplace to view modern jazz as a logical outgrowth of the past, an evolution rather than a revolution. Hindsight is a great peacemaker, especially since no one can mistake the obvious debts Parker, Gillespie, Monk, and Clark owed such predecessors as Young, Eldridge, Teddy Wilson, and Jo Jones. Yet war there was. In the period of genesis, sides were drawn and barbs were traded. Some of the animosity stemmed from the exclusionary practices at those fevered jam sessions, even though they were implemented not to foment a generation gap, but to discourage second-raters. Although dull critics and promoters continued to revile bop, older musicians soon realized that the prank-happy beboppers were a little more than kin, if less than kind. Howard McGhee, one of the music's earliest disciples, makes the point in an illustrative anecdote: "When Bird first came on the scene, I asked Johnny Hodges, 'What do you think of Charlie Parker?' He said, 'He don't play nothing, he ain't got no sound.' Later when I got a chance to play with Ellington, I asked him again. 'Oh, he was beautiful.' 'But Johnny, you told me he didn't have no sound.' 'Well, I didn't know what I was talking about.'" Of course, Parker had no such ambivalence about Hodges's matchless, sculptural sound. He called him "Johnny Lily Pons Hodges . . . cause he can *sing* with the horn."

When McShann took the band back to Kansas City on a tour, Parker chose to stay in New York, and became actively involved in the sessions at Minton's and elsewhere. Mary Lou Williams, living at a hotel in Dewey Square, had created a kind of salon for young musicians. Informal workshops proliferated, so that ideas could be exchanged in private and then tested in public. Parker's arrival in New York was a revelation to the easterners. His music was integrated and authoritative, his "sanctified sound" (in Gillespie's phrase) an entity beyond the uncertainty of experimentation. Having done most of his laboratory work in Kansas City, while Gillespie and Monk were exchanging ideas in New York, he

Thelonious Monk at Minton's Playhouse, New York City, 1947.

6 7

Bud Powell at the Open Door, New York City, 1953.

appeared on the scene with a finished product. According to Gillespie, "Charlie Parker was the architect of the new sound. He knew how to get from one note to another, the style of the thing. Most of what I did was in the area of harmony and rhythm." It remained for the other musicians in the ensemble to adapt Parker's precepts.

Duke Ellington's renowned trumpet soloist Cootie Williams once called Parker "the greatest individual musician that ever lived," justifying his claim with the observation that "every instrument in the band tried to copy Charlie Parker, and in the history of jazz there had never been one man who influenced all the instruments."[*] His influence was felt immediately. Kenny Clarke and a magnificent teenage drummer from Brooklyn, Max Roach, shifted rhythmic accents from the skins to the cymbals, replacing the thud-thud-thud of the bass drum with the sibilant pulse of the ride cymbal. Oscar Pettiford, picking up where Duke Ellington's bassist Jimmy Blanton left off, showed how the bass could provide a melodic counterpoint to the primary solos, rather than the usual cycle of tonic notes. Bud Powell exemplified the new role of the pianist, who no longer replicated the full-bodied dimension of an orchestra, but pared down his accompaniment to a brisk, jagged series of chords and soloed with the linearity of a wind instrument. All wind instrumentalists—including, during the next few years, such influential figures as Dexter Gordon and Stan Getz on tenor sax, J. J. Johnson on trombone, Fats Navarro on trumpet, and Buddy DeFranco on clarinet—emulated Parker's vibratoless, unmannered tonal production, his rhythmic and harmonic values, and his emphatically emotional ideas that transcended ground rhythms and chords and attempted to bring the listener into a deeper communion with the music.

All the while, Parker continued in his erratic relationship with McShann. There were memorable nights, such as the broadcast in Baltimore when Parker's "Cherokee" choruses so excited the announcer that he let the band play overtime. But there were dissatisfactions on both sides. Bird occasionally asked Buddy Tate to get him into the Basie band. "Man," he'd tell Tate, "I'm from Kansas City and I should be in there." At that time Basie had only four reeds, and Tate argued Parker's case: "He's playing something different and he wants to come in tomorrow." Basie's rejoinder was, "I know he can play, but he looks so bad." When his lead alto, Earle Warren, was out for a minor operation, Basie and Tate went to hear Parker on what turned out to be a sorrowful night. He not only looked disheveled—wearing loud, fireman's

*In an unpublished interview with Helen Oakley Dance for the oral-history program of the Institute of Jazz Studies, Rutgers.

suspenders and trousers inches short of his ankles—but got sick onstage. The job went to Tab Smith.

Parker's time with McShann ended abruptly while the band was on tour. McShann had tried to keep the pushers away from Bird, and Gene Ramey had taken it upon himself to look out for him and see that he showed up straight and on time. Their best efforts were subverted when the band arrived at the Paradise Theater in Detroit. As Parker walked falteringly to the mike for his first solo, the audience broke into laughter. McShann peered over and saw he wasn't wearing shoes. Parker had overdosed. When he recuperated he took a job with Andy Kirk's band, also playing Detroit, to get passage back to New York. In Lansing, Michigan, Big Nick Nicholas was in the audience to hear Kirk, and he remembers Bird playing "Indian Summer" so fast that his father, also a saxophonist, commented, "He sounds like a machine." Backstage, Parker let Nick play his alto and taught him Monk's "Epistrophy."

Earl Hines had expressed interest in hiring Charlie, had even kidded McShann that he could "make a man of him." He got his chance in December 1942, when with the help of Billy Eckstine and Benny Harris, he convinced Bird to take over Budd Johnson's chair and play tenor. (The alto chairs were already occupied by Scoops Carey and an old acquaintance, Goon Gardner.) Within a couple of months, Hines griped to McShann that the in-

Charlie Rouse, Ernie Henry, Tadd Dameron, Theodore "Fats" Navarro, New York City, 1947.

corrigible Bird owed money to everyone in the band and every loan shark in town, and missed more than his share of shows. He also expressed amazement at Parker's ability to memorize an arrangement after a single reading. For Parker, the eight-month period with Hines meant a chance to get closer to Gillespie, Harris, and other modernists in the band, including Sarah Vaughan, who was signed after she won an amateur contest at the Apollo Theater and was mesmerized by Parker's music. It also provided him with a chance to beat the Petrillo recording ban, though few people would know about it until forty-three years later.

In February 1943, while the band played Chicago, Eckstine introduced Parker to his friend and sometime valet and driver, Bob Redcross, who organized jam sessions in his room at the Savoy Hotel. Using a Silvertone disc recorder, which he learned to master while monitoring radio airchecks, Redcross documented those sessions. Rumors circulated about the discs for decades, for only a small circle of friends knew about them. As late as 1974, a standard Parker discography listed them as "unknown titles" recorded at the Ritz Hotel for the American Red Cross. When he noticed the wax beginning to flake, Redcross wrapped the discs in a 1949 issue of *The Chicago Tribune* and stored them until 1985, when steps were taken to issue them on an album. As the only samples of Parker's playing during a crucial period of twenty-six months, they are most illuminating. Performances include "Sweet Georgia Brown," the first recorded joust—nearly eight minutes long—between Parker and Gillespie, accompanied by Oscar Pettiford's bass; the first of many Parker variations on "Embraceable You," played as a duet with Hazel Scott's 1942 Decca recording; an improvisation on "I Got Rhythm" chords in which Parker quotes Ben Webster's famous "Cottontail" solo and previews the rhythmic riff that Tiny Grimes and Parker later recorded as "Red Cross"; and versions of "Boogie Woogie" and "Indiana" that intimate Parker's musical antecedents even as they unveil bop licks that wouldn't gain general currency for another two years.

On April 10, 1943, while the Hines band was on tour in Washington, D.C., Parker married Geraldine Marguerite Scott, a dancer and the only one of his wives who he allowed to dabble in drugs. As she later remarked, "When I met him, all he had was a horn and a habit. He gave me the habit." The marriage lasted about a year, although no record of their divorce was ever found. Little is known about her other than that she was subsequently jailed on a narcotics charge and died in New Jersey in the early 1980s. But Parker's insouciance about ending the marriage echoed some of the ugliness surrounding his break with Rebecca and presaged the complications that would plague his estate. He was ailing and

Opposite page: Charlie Parker at the home of William Claxton, the photographer, then a teenager, who had invited Parker to stay with him while his parents were away for the weekend. Pasadena, California, June 1953.
Below: Geraldine Scott Parker.

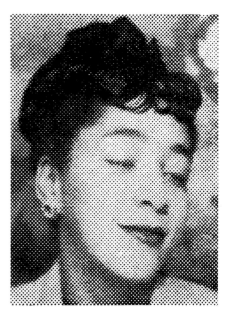

tired and moving too fast. His restlessness reflected turmoil in the Hines band, itself in a state of revolt. When Eckstine quit with the idea of forming his own orchestra, eight musicians left with him—the modernist contingent. Dizzy stayed in New York while they waited for Eckstine to organize, but Charlie returned to his mother's house in Kansas City. Once again he worked for Tootie Clarkin in a Missouri suburb, while the new music was about to find a New York home.

In the years immediately following Kansas City's decline as a mecca for jazz, no community offered nearly as prestigious and electrifying a substitute as the strip of brownstones on New York's Fifty-second Street, between Fifth and Sixth Avenues. Known simply as The Street, it was a banquet of small clubs, bars, and restaurants snuggled one against the other, presenting jazz, pop, comedy, and dancing. Budd Johnson, a tireless activist for venturesome jazz, helped to get some of the younger players employed there. In early 1944, with the recording ban over, he organized a historic record session for Coleman Hawkins which featured Gillespie (his writing as well as his playing) and employed Pettiford, Leo Parker (no relation to Charlie), and, in his recording debut, Max Roach. Bird was represented in absentia with a lick from "The Jumpin' Blues" that Dizzy scored behind Hawkins's solo on "Disorder at the Border." Two months later, while Charlie was still in Kansas City, Eckstine recorded with a big studio band that included Gillespie (his musical director), Budd, Freddie Webster, Wardell Gray, Clyde Hart, Pettiford, and Shadow Wilson. With the success of those records, Eckstine was able to secure financial backing to form his orchestra.

Eckstine located Parker in Chicago, where he'd gone to play a job with Noble Sissle, and asked him to take charge of the reed section. At first Parker took to his position eagerly, hiring Gene Ammons on tenor and Leo Parker on baritone. Onstage, he continued to dazzle listeners with countless choruses of "Cherokee," as well as a new piece by Gillespie, "Max Is Making Wax," and ballads with Sarah Vaughan. After a while, though, he handed in his notice, complaining that his lack of discipline was too much of a liability for the band. Eckstine refused to let him go, and in the fall the band whipped itself into shape during a two-week stay at the Riviera Club in St. Louis, where eighteen-year-old Miles Davis, more enthusiastic than proficient, sat in. In her interview with Reisner, Addie Parker says that it was during that job that Parker wired Rebecca to join him and asked to remarry her. Rebecca insists that the incident took place a few years earlier, but since she also recalls that Parker was playing with Eckstine and that Miles Davis was in attendance, the earlier date seems unlikely. In any case, Charlie sent Rebecca a ticket and asked her

Billy Eckstine and Sarah Vaughn, 1947.

to meet him in St. Louis, where he lodged her in a different hotel than the one where the band boarded. He gave her his key to the Olive Steet house. It was his way of breaking off with Kansas City, since he couldn't bring himself to say good-bye to Addie.

Rebecca never considered returning to him. By this time her life had been thrown into more turmoil than Charlie knew. Sometime after he had asked for their divorce, her brother Winfrey brought her and Leon back to Fanny Ruffin's house in Leeds, a district of Kansas City. Months later they learned that Addie had gone to Leeds to lodge a complaint against Rebecca for living with a man. It was her first blow in a custody battle over Leon. Winfrey and Rebecca were employed respectively by the Juvenile Authority and the National Youth Administration. She was too well known for the accusation to stick. Nevertheless, a judge put Leon in Fanny's care for six months, and issued an ultimatum that Rebecca obtain her divorce from Charlie and remarry. Rebecca was outraged, but Fanny overruled her objections. She found someone who could obtain the divorce for twenty-five dollars and arranged a marriage that lasted just long enough for Rebecca to secure custody of her son. Charlie never knew about any of this, she says. Nor was he much interested; he rarely paid alimony or child support. He had a new life now in New York, intensified not only by his steadily escalating coterie, but by a personal sway far beyond his years. Always an expert mimic, he even spoke differently in New York, occasionally affecting Oxfordian plum tones. In divesting himself of his house key, he made the symbolic break that he hoped would deliver him the world.

(Left to right) 1st row: Dizzy Gillespie, Benny Harris, Gail Brockman, Shorty McConnell, Earl Hines, Sarah Vaughn, A. Crump, Andy "Goon" Gardner, George "Scoops" Carry, John Williams, Charlie Parker; 2nd row: Benny Green, Gus Chappell, Howard Scott, Shadow Wilson, Jesse Simpkins, Clifton "Skeeter" Best, Julie Gardner, at the Apollo Theatre, New York City, April 23, 1943.

. . . .

Fifty-second Street, looking east from Sixth Avenue,
1948.

. . . .

7 4

4

MASTERY

❦ ❦ ❦ ❦ ❦ ❦

THE SECOND WORLD WAR severely altered the texture and tempo of American life, and jazz reflected those changes with greater acuteness by far than the other arts, with the arguable exception of painting. Popular music was pervaded by canned patriotism, sentimental bromides, and silly novelties. Hollywood's conduit for benedictions was Bing Crosby dressed as a priest. Broadway looked backward even when it was serious (*The Glass Menagerie, The Skin of Our Teeth*), though it preferred outright nostalgia (*I Remember Mama, Life With Father*). A popular appetite for poetry was requited by a potential law firm of the trade: Benét, Benét, Millay, McGinley, and Nash. Though the novel fared better, most especially in the South, only Richard Wright's *Native Son* successfully broached the agenda of race, which remained on the back burner until thousands of returning black servicemen who helped save the world for democracy demanded a little of the same. Still, it was the new jazz that set the most comprehensive tone for black discontent and black accomplishment, tempering anger with ebullience, sorrow with nobility, hurt with beauty, impudence with genius. Parker, Gillespie, and Monk were of the first generation born during the Harlem renaissance. History was on their side and they knew it. The world could not fail to take notice of their music.

One elemental difference between popular and serious art is that the former gives society what it wants and the latter gives it what it must. The impact modern jazz had on American life is reflected not least in the number of people, including countless artists in other fields, who found themselves relearning their responses to music because of it. Indeed, bebop's glittery blare reawakened many to the astonishing fact that much of what was best in American culture emerged from a formerly enslaved and often despised minority. Which is not to say that its proponents achieved a level of mastery or seriousness lacking in their pred-

Opposite page: Charlie Parker, Tommy Potter, c. 1950.

ecessors. The music of Armstrong, Ellington, Bessie Smith, Hawkins, Young, Holiday, Basie, Tatum, Eldridge, and many others of the 1920s and 1930s was every bit as expert, personal, and willful. The choices they made were in all important respects exclusively musical, even in the face of commercial concessions. Yet they represented the first wave of accomplishment, when jazz and popular music could reinforce each other; the modernists knew that that marriage was no longer tenable. Jazz in the Swing Era was so frequently compromised by chuckleheaded bandleaders, most of them white, who diluted and undermined the triumphs of serious musicians that a new virtuosity was essential. The modernists brandished it like a weapon. They confronted social and musical complacency in a spirit of arrogant romanticism. Their art was a relentless celebration of self.

That modern jazz disenfranchised conservative listeners no one can doubt. Yet its leaders were not the sort of apostates who thrive as a clique, snubbing bourgeois acceptance. They were pioneers who cultivated an audience on their own terms. "Don't play what the public wants," Monk advised, "you play what you want and let the public pick up on what you are doing—even if it does take them fifteen, twenty years." Monk eventually found an audience, as Gillespie had before him, as Parker did posthumously. It was natural for Gilllespie to exploit the publicity value of bebop-rebop-hipster jive, which Parker disdained. ("Let's not call it bebop. Let's call it music," he pleaded.) But Parker was no less intent on securing approval. His insistence on performing with an ensemble of strings betrayed less of a debt to Stravinsky and Hindemith than to the sugary backdrops Armstrong favored for his interpretations of pop songs nearly twenty years earlier. Yet he was accused of alienating the jazz following, of scorning dancers and entertainment values.

The truth is a bit more complicated. After all, Parker paid his dues in dance bands, admired great dancers (he named Baby Laurence as an influence), and relished those rare opportunities when he could play ballrooms. He was himself a good dancer, like Gillespie, who, at sixty-nine, still cuts a rug onstage. (Monk also danced onstage, though his terpsichorean skills were somewhat more eccentric.) The idea that modernists spurned dance is as fallacious as the idea that swing bands played entirely for lindy hoppers. Even Glenn Miller, a singularly astute judge of pop fashions, confided to a colleague that he sometimes brightened his tempos to force dancers to stand still and listen. Still, as a head music, modern jazz contributed—along with the war, cabaret laws, inflation, television, and rock and roll, all of which combined to destroy big bands, ballrooms, and night life—to the ultimate split between jazz and coloquial dance.

Modernism's presumed rejection of entertainment values also requires a closer look. Gillespie, a natural comedian, is the best-known jazz clown since Armstrong and Waller. Parker was no less ready to demonstrate antic wit and irreverence, albeit in a strictly musical context. Gillespie speaks often of how funny "Yard" could be. In the 1945 recording of "Warming Up a Riff," we hear Gillespie guffaw at Parker's outlandish digression into inapposite song fragments. Significantly, Parker didn't know the performance was being recorded. Yet this is the sort of thing he did nightly to regale musicians and listeners. At black theaters around the country, he was known to sing, joke, and encourage congregational responses to his musical sermons. The distancing effect of modern jazz stemmed not from any desire to estrange audiences, but from difficulties inherent in a music that, for all its emotional qualities, demanded concentration and empathy. The new jazz could not be apprehended entirely through toe-tap-

At a recording session in New York City by Sir Charles and His All Stars: (left to right) Sir Charles Thompson, Jimmy Butts, Dexter Gordon, Buck Clayton, J.C. Heard, Danny Barker, Charlie Parker, September 4, 1945.

ping physical responses—not in the 1940s, anyway. When a generation of disciples eventually turned Parker's innovations into maxims, the music was forced to take far more drastic steps to force an intellectual response. Within fifteen years jazz was ready to jettison all the familiar signposts: countable time, chord changes, even the tempered scale. But that's another story, almost another world.

In 1944, the jazz audience could still be riled by a flatted fifth—an interval (for example, F-sharp against C-natural) found useful for suggesting bitonality, which soon became just another blue note. At the outset of bop, it was considered a terrible dissonance, a symptom of modern jazz's frantic assault on decency and good taste. Consequently, no nightclub booking in jazz history sparked more anticipation or controversy than the long-awaited teaming of Diz and Bird on Fifty-second Street. At long last, the music was coming out of hiding. Gillespie had already paved the way. After leaving Eckstine's band (he brought in Fats Navarro as his replacement), he teamed with Oscar Pettiford to lead a band at the Onyx, with pianist George Wallington, tenor saxophonist Don Byas, and Roach. He had wired Parker in Kansas City to join them, but the telegram wasn't received. Parker had also left Eckstine (John Jackson was his replacement) and soon made his debut on The Street in a group led by Ben Webster. Then Sammy Kaye, the owner of the Three Deuces, a narrow little club just off Sixth Avenue, decided to hire the founders of the new movement for an eight-week stint. Gillespie was the contractor and leader. He hired drummer Stan Levey (Roach was touring with Benny Carter), bassist Curly Russell, and (because Bud Powell was unavailable) a gifted pianist from Newark, Al Haig, who showed an immediate receptivity to their music. They rehearsed afternoons, either at the Deuces or Gillespie's home. When they opened, with Erroll Garner playing intermission piano, they established bop as a permanent item on The Street's bill of fare.

With a seating capacity of about 125, the Deuces was usually packed. Many listeners admitted they didn't understand the new music, with its furious, barbed ensemble themes and flaring solos, but they found it enticing all the same and came back for more. The responsiveness between Parker and Gillespie was unlike anything heard in jazz since the early twenties, when King Oliver and Louis Armstrong crossed trumpets at Chicago's Lincoln Gardens. Occasionally, they seemed to ad lib theme statements in perfect unison, and their reeling exchanges of four- and eight-bar passages brought time to a stop and audiences to a roar. Parker didn't always show up on time—or at all—but when he hit the stand his playing was amazingly consistent. On an average night as many as a dozen ace bands would be playing The Street,

Opposite page: Charlie Parker at the Three Deuces, New York City, 1948.

. . . .

Charlie Parker, Tommy Potter, Dizzy Gillespie,
at Birdland, New York City, 1951.

· · · · · · · · · · ·

8 2

The house that 'Bop' built...

(Left to right) Milt Jackson, Al Haig, unknown, Charlie Parker, Nicole Barclay, Max Roach, Mrs. Kenny Dorham, Kenny Dorham, at the Royal Roost, New York City, 1949.

and most of the musicians eventually dropped in at the Deuces, or sidled over to Bird at the White Rose, where they relaxed between shows. Looking back, few of them can believe Bird was not yet twenty-five; there was a luminous, aged quality about him. He magnetized people. His beguiling charm and gold-toothed smile increased his circle of converts nightly, and the rumored disparity between his erratic life and his brilliance onstage was mere grist for the legend aborning.

Bird flourished in the bustling, integrated atmosphere of The

Street, engorging himself with drugs, women, drink, food, and music in any order they came. His appetite for life exhilarated his friends, and made him an easy mark for the parasites and pushers who dogged his steps as relentlessly as his fans. With mobsters like Frank Costello running things, Fifty-second Street was something of a safe house from the police, though not from such peculiarly American treacheries as white servicemen who taunted black musicians on the stand on in the bars, especially when they were in the company of white women. For the most part, however, New York was a movable feast, and Bird tasted of it fully, fusing with people of every sort and storing motley bits of information. He seemed to know something about everything, from science to chess to politics. Just as you could never tell what he would play from set to set, you couldn't predict where his conversation would turn. He had a way of discerning the subjects that were of interest to people, especially his young admirers. "He spoke beautifully and he was very kind," Al Cohn says. "He could talk to intellectuals about music and art and turn around and talk to street people as though he were one of them." Pepper Adams was only sixteen when he met him in Detroit and they became friends because of a mutual fascination with Honegger. When Bird's opinions appeared in print, young fans sprang into action. "After I read that he liked Schönberg," Phil Woods recalls, "I started to listen to Schönberg. Whatever Bird said, that was it, you had to check it out."

Yet his habit worsened, and his absences increased to the point that Gillespie was regularly making excuses and carrying the show. Genius doesn't know its own worth, Sartre has written. By all accounts, Bird knew his, but the knowledge was never enough to still the demons. One night Gillespie unwittingly incited a rift between them. As Curly Russell described the incident to Crouch, Bird arrived late and locked himself in the john. After a long while, Gillespie angrily told Roach that Parker was in there with a needle in his arm. Gillespie didn't realize he was standing next to an open mike. Everyone in the room heard him, including Parker, who felt betrayed. Yet despite his illness, he not only continued at the Deuces but jammed down the street at Tondelayo's, where guitarist Tiny Grimes had a band. As far as Grimes was concerned, Bird "couldn't be beat. No problem, no arguments, no nothing. He was glad to play and I played everything that I could to back him up." He showed up so often that they worked out head arrangements. When Grimes was asked to record for Savoy, he naturally called Parker.

The session with Grimes (in September of 1944) was the first of seven that Parker made in the course of a year, all as a sideman. It was his first time in a studio in two years—since McShann—· · · · · · · · · · ·

Charlie Parker at the Three Deuces, New York City, 1948.

and though the context was swing rather than bop, the maturity of Parker's sound was unmistakable. Of the four pieces, two were Grimes vocals, supported by Parker's fluent obbligato, and two were instrumentals that demonstrated Bird's incomparable affinity for the basic song structures he played unswervingly throughout his life: the twelve-bar blues ("Tiny's Tempo") and the thirty-two-bar pop song with "I Got Rhythm" harmonies ("Red Cross"). His loyalty to those foundations, notwithstanding his dauntless chord substitutions, is one of the enduring ironies of Parker's music. On "Red Cross," he employed the mop-mop figure (named for the quarter-notes played on the first two beats of a bar, followed by a two-beat rest) he'd played in Bob Redcross's hotel room.

The next session, with Clyde Hart's All Stars, was another transitional date with swing and bop players (including Dizzy), and is best remembered for the strange vocals by Rubberlegs Wil-

liams, who a few moments before recording accidentally drank
Bird's coffee rather than his own. Bird's was heavily spiked with
benzedrine. Parker and Gillespie also appeared on sessions led by
pianist Sir Charles Thompson ("The Street Beat" was yet another
mop-mop variant) and vibraphonist Red Norvo ("Hallelujah" has
an impressive Parker solo on a tune he'd practiced with Biddy
Fleet). Of greater significance were one session with Sarah
Vaughan (Roach and Dameron participated) and two with Gillespie. Despite the presence of swing drummers, Dizzy's sessions for
Guild firmly established the new style on records: the original
pieces became classics of the repertory—"Groovin' High," "Dizzy
Atmosphere," "Salt Peanuts," "Shaw Nuff," and "Hot House," all
based on the blueprints of pop songs. Finally, on November 26,
1945, Parker was signed for his own session on Savoy.

It's not difficult to perceive the original impact of "Ko Ko." To
this day, four decades later, unprepared listeners often respond to
it in much the same way—as an explosion of sound, a mad

At Massey Hall, Toronto: Dizzy Gillespie and Charlie
Parker (with plastic alto), May 1953.

. . . .

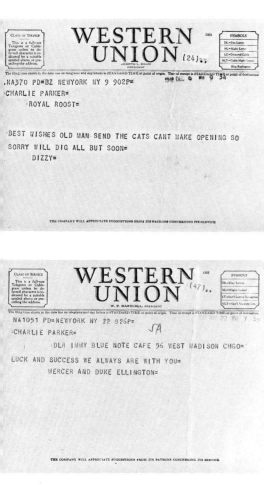

WESTERN
UNION (24).

NA370 PD=BZ NEWYORK NY 9 902P=
CHARLIE PARKER=
ROYAL ROOST=

BEST WISHES OLD MAN SEND THE CATS CANT MAKE OPENING SO
SORRY WILL DIG ALL BUT SOON=
DIZZY=

WESTERN
UNION (47).

NA1051 PD=NEWYORK NY 22 826P=
CHARLIE PARKER=
DLR IMMY BLUE NOTE CAFE 56 WEST MADISON CHGO=
LUCK AND SUCCESS WE ALWAYS ARE WITH YOU=
MERCER AND DUKE ELLINGTON=

Above: Telegrams from Dizzy Gillespie and Mercer
and Duke Ellington.
Opposite page: Charlie Parker, c. 1947.

scramble of notes. Only on repeated listenings are the logic and coherence—the melodies—revealed. Based on the chords of "Cherokee," the specialty feature of Parker's apprenticeship, "Ko Ko" was the seminal point of departure for jazz in the postwar era. Its effect paralleled that of Armstrong's "West End Blues" in 1928. Armstrong began with a clarion cadenza; "Ko Ko" opens with an equivalent jolt—a blistering eight-bar unison theme of daunting virtuosity, coupled with improvised eight-bar arabesques by Parker and Gillespie. Then Parker takes off for two choruses of overwhelming originality, as though he were putting everything he knew into this one performance, imposing his will on the music and the musicians, setting forth new precepts with redoubtable nerve. Though improvised at tremendous velocity, his solo is colored with deft conceits: the clanging riff in the first eight bars, the casual reference to "High Society" at the outset of the second chorus, the chromatic arpeggios in the release. And his sound!—so deeply, profoundly human; fat and sensuous, yet jagged and hard; inflamed with a gleeful audacity. Braced by the cold winds of Max Roach's drums, "Ko Ko" struck with the violence and calm of a hurricane. In a word, it was thrilling.

Yet "Ko Ko" capped an oddly bedeviled session. Parker had agreed to record two blues and variants on "Cherokee" and "I Got Rhythm" with a quintet that included Bud Powell and Miles Davis. At the last minute, Powell couldn't make it, so Bird brought Dizzy and Argonne Thronton (aka Sadik Hakim), who had neither a union card nor a firm grasp of modern piano. Bird was plagued with reed problems and Davis had difficulties with the themes, which Parker notated shortly before the session. Still, they recorded two classic F major blues, "Billie's Bounce" and "Now's the Time,"* with Parker solos that were dissected and imitated for years. On "Now's the Time," backed by Gillespie's provoking piano chords, Parker's phrases erupt upredictably, yet with inviolable poise. His melodic figures bleed new life into the most basic of jazz songs. Davis's chorus hasn't much rhythmic interest, but he employs a broad sound and advanced harmonies to fix a memorable melodic response, in the manner of his friend Freddie Webster. Parker also extemporized on the chords of "Embraceable You" ("Meandering"), "I Got Rhythm" ("Thriving on a Riff"), and "Cherokee" ("Warming Up a Riff"). By the time he was ready to tackle the final version of "Cherokee" ("Ko Ko")—after a frenzied hunt for new reeds—Davis had passed out and

*They were not greeted as potential classics at the time. A *Down Beat* reviewer excoriated them for reflecting the "bad taste and ill-advised fanaticism of Dizzy's uninhibited style," which he dismissed as "the sort of stuff that has thrown innumerable impressionable young musicians out of stride, that has harmed many of them irreparably."

(Left to right) Doris Parker, Charlie Parker, Dizzy Gillespie, Jerry Lester (television host, Broadway Open House), New York City, January 1949.

Dizzy, assisted by Thornton, doubled on trumpet and piano. At first Parker intended to use the actual melody of "Cherokee," but no sooner did they start to play than he changed his mind. Whether he discarded it to avoid a copyright dispute or because it took too long to play or because he realized—as the listener, hearing the false take, is bound to realize—that it simply didn't belong, his decision helped to confirm jazz's emergence from the shadows of Tin Pan Alley tunesmiths. Ironically, this assault on jazz conventions also proved his parting shot to New York for two years.

Two weeks later Parker left with Gillespie for an engagement in Los Angeles. He probably relished the change in scenery. For several months now his life had mirrored the disorganization of his first record date. He had taken up with both of the women who would play prominent roles in his remaining years. Chan Richardson (the stage name of Beverly Berg) was a flamboyant ex-dancer who had been bred on the fringes of show business. Her mother, with whom she shared a brownstone on The Street, had been a Ziegfeld girl, and they created a casual salon for musicians. Doris Sydnor, a gangly, unassuming midwesterner, worked as a hatcheck girl at the Spotlite and was introduced to Bird by the violinist Stuff Smith. Although he dated Chan, he moved in with Doris. Bird had been boarding all over town, most recently with Miles Davis, who came to New York at eighteen for the stated purpose of studying at Juilliard and the secret purpose of studying with Bird. Davis not only invited Parker to live with him, but gave him a weekly percentage of his allowance. Parker took him under his wing, introduced him to the practice sessions at Dizzy's house and the ways of The Street, and hired him for a gig at the Deuces after Dizzy left the quintet to start a big band. Their friendship was edgy, however, and gradually, almost imperceptibly, Bird began moving his belongings into Doris's apartment on 117th Street and Manhattan Avenue. The first time she walked in on him while he was shooting up, she got sick, but eventually she grew used to it. She loved him and, not realizing the full potency of his habit, only that he seemed more in control of it than he was of liquor, she accepted it.

By late 1945, mobster primacy on The Street was under seige by the vice squad, for reasons similar to those that closed New Orleans's fabled Storyville district. Too many servicemen were getting into trouble, and the military demanded a crackdown. Many of the downtown clubs were shuttered, some for good, and musicians were scrambling for work. A deal was struck: Gillespie would bring a sextet to Billy Berg's in Los Angeles. Bird would be featured, but vibraharpist Milt Jackson would also be along in case Parker missed a gig. As it happened, he missed so many that Lucky Thompson was recruited to fill out the band. Desperately in need of heroin, settling for inferior goods that frayed his nerves and wore him down, Parker soon took the fall he had postponed for nearly a decade. Out west, he suddenly learned how strung out he was. Yet he didn't come apart at once. The Los Angeles nightmare began disarmingly enough, then reached the panic stage familiar to all addicts, and finally turned to horror as he found himself pressed hopelessly at the cliff's edge.

Before he jumped, Parker had his triumphs. A few months earlier, Howard McGhee had brought the new music to the coast, and a generation of young musicians—Dexter Gordon, Art Pepper, Hampton Hawes, Wardell Gray, Jimmy Knepper, Sonny Criss, Gerald Wilson, Chico Hamilton, among dozens of others, including virtually the entire personnel of Stan Kenton's orchestra—was in tune with it. For them the arrival of Bird and Diz was cause for celebration, and opening night at Billy Berg's was likened by some to the debut of *The Rite of Spring*. That comparison was validated by the response of patrons who tittered derisively from the opening notes, disdainful critics, and a few commissars of radio, who pronounced the music "degenerate" and banned it from the air. It was heard nevertheless, on radio broadcasts (some of them sponsored by the Armed Forces Radio Service) and records (including a jocular session with Slim Gaillard, the jivey singer and pianist), and at the *Jazz at the Philharmonic* concert series. JATP

Pincus the doorman, who became known as "the Mayor" of Fifty-second Street, New York City, 1948.

(Left to right) Charlie Parker, Harry Babison, Chet Baker, Helen Carr, at the Tiffany Club, Los Angeles, California, June 1953.

put Dizzy and Bird on the same stage as Lester Young and Willie Smith, and it's difficult to imagine how anyone hearing Gillespie's magnificent rendering of "The Man I Love" or Parker's sweeping descants on "Sweet Georgia Brown" could have questioned their legitimacy.

Ross Russell, the proprietor of a local record shop and a small label called Dial, signed the easterners for a recording session. After completing one number, "Diggin' Diz," Parker disappeared. The band recorded a second session without him and, after a fruitless search for the wayward Bird, returned to New York. It was later learned that he had cashed in his plane ticket and gone on a binge. Why he chose to strand himself in a hostile city without a job is a mystery. He became dependent on a paraplegic pusher known as Moose the Mooche, who made his way to the clubs in a wheelchair. While the heroin was forthcoming, he was able to take care of business. Miles Davis was there, having traveled west with Benny Carter's Los Angeles-based band, so Bird formed a rhythm section and found the quintet work at the Finale Club. He also appeared with *Jazz at the Philharmonic* again. At the March 25, 1946, concert, Parker played one of his most influential solos in a performance of "Lady Be Good" alongside Lester Young. Entering on the heels of a Teddy Wilson-inspired piano solo by Arnold Ross, Bird delivers two choruses that alchemize the Gershwin ballad into a near-feral blues. Although he actually plays the first four notes of the melody, he voices them with such ardent command that the phrase is transfigured into a plea far more impassioned than anything the mincing lyric could suggest. The first salvo is sustained, variations develop sui generis. Every aspect of the solo became part of the grammar of modern jazz. Indeed, his trenchant ideas were so widely imitated that Young's subsequent solo, one of his most imaginative of the period, was generally overlooked.*

Three days later Bird led his first session at Dial, a *tour de force*. Driving to the studio, with drummer Roy Porter at the wheel, he composed a tribute to his connection, "Moose the Mooche," an upbeat theme on which he improvised a sly, economic chorus that peaks with a quotation from Hawkins's "Body and Soul." He also unveiled his winsome melody from 1941, "Yardbird Suite"; Benny Harris's expansion of his early blues lick, "Ornithology"; and Gillespie's exotic "A Night in Tunisia." On the last, Parker played an involuted four-bar break of baroque complexity and numbing speed. The rhythm section was stymied, unable to coordinate its reentry. On subsequent takes, Davis had to

---

*Though not by King Pleasure, who lyricised its haunting melodic figures in a song he called "Golden Days." Eddie Jefferson wrote a lyric to Parker's solo and called it "Disappointed."

walk to the side, count the measures, and conduct. Bird's exultation was short-lived. Uneasy about sustaining a source of drugs, he signed over half his royalties to the Mooche, who was arrested in April. He drank heavily, lived in a converted garage. Only six months had passed since "Ko Ko," and Charlie Parker was coming apart at the seams.

Howard McGhee found him work and, in July, helped organize the Dial session that all too vividly documented his collapse. Parker's sound is parched, his articulation blurred, his timing inchoate. On "Lover Man," he founders in shallow waters, tossing in dilatory confusion as though the shore were always one stroke beyond his grasp. Yet the performance is oddly indigenous and moving. When Russell released it, an indiscretion for which Bird never forgave him, callow musicians memorized it, mistakes and all. After a disastrous attempt at a fast piece, he crumpled into a chair. That night at the Civic Hotel he twice wandered into the lobby naked. Later he fell asleep smoking a cigarette, which ignited his mattress. Despite billowing smoke and braying sirens, the fire fighters had to roust him from sleep. When he protested, the police blackjacked and handcuffed him. They jailed him for ten days, until Russell was able to have him transferred to Camarillo State Hospital, where he was incarcerated for the next six months. He emerged in the winter of 1947, temporarily reformed.

Charlie Parker and two fans at the Tiffany Club, Los Angeles, California, June 1953.

BIRD LIVES

❧   ❧   ❧   ❧   ❧   ❧

THE RESTORED, REVITALIZED Charlie Parker of 1947 is the public Bird, the Bird of a thousand acquaintances, of numberless funny and harrowing anecdotes, of a profusion of masterpieces. The period of his ascension dates from his triumphant return to New York in April to his deliverance eight years later, and is chronicled in passionate, contradictory, wistful testimonies. Like loosely assembled fragments of a shattered mirror, they reflect a huge, tremulous mosaic. The image looms elusively, adopting a different temper with every ray of light. Even the photographs are a magic show. His weight billows and recedes, his face—a potato from one perspective, a stone carving from another—transmogrifies as the boyish spark is quenched and revived. Only the eyes are candid, registering cockiness, intensity, wit, detachment, pain, pleasure, concentration, anger, and more. The premature creases speak less of sickness and self-abuse than of a life that never knew youth, yet sustained the veneer of youth to cloak unseasonable knowledge. (Rebecca: "Charlie was always old." Chan: "I couldn't believe he was just twenty-six.") He might almost have been born with the authority of a sachem.

The music, too, defies easy apprehension. Only in jazz is the official work frequently qualified by ancillary discoveries. Sketches do not supersede the painting, first drafts do not supplant the published novel or musical score. But jazz records—the art's one covenant with posterity—are definitive only by default. They document random performances, especially in the case of a musician as committed to improvisation as Bird. Even a cursory examination of his alternate takes shows the degree of serendipity involved in producing work that is soon considered classic. How many thousands of potential classics, then, were performed in the absence of recording engineers? Beginning with his 1947 homecoming, sixty pounds heavier and lustrous with good health, Parker was stalked by amateur recordists intent on preserving

Opposite page: Tommy Potter, Charlie Parker, Max Roach, at the Three Deuces, New York City, 1948.

(Left to right) Charles Mingus, Charlie Parker, Symphony Sid Torin at Birdland, New York City, 1953.

every fugitive solo. Single-minded and thrifty, they recorded Parker exclusively, turning off the disc, wire, or tape machines when other members of his band soloed. Some documented radio airchecks, others followed him into clubs, still others had access to private jam sessions. The technology that domesticated entertainment makes every consumer a potential producer. Leaving aside the issue of theft, which remains thorny because American copyright laws are stubbornly inhospitable to improvised music, those low-fidelity mementos vastly enlarge our understanding of Parker's accomplishment.

More than 350 Parker improvisations recorded privately between 1947 and 1954 (*excluding* posthumously discovered studio performances) have surfaced in the thirty years since his death, and they constitute a treasure with few parallels in musical history. (One thinks of Ellington in our time, and of the manuscripts in Schubert's attic.) They afford us far more than extended solos or versions of compositions that he never officially recorded, and substantiate the claims of his contemporaries, who insist that the records, magnificent though they are, do not tell the whole story. They are proof that the formalist, who structures his inventions with sovereign care in the confines of a three-minute 78 RPM record, raged luminously, almost recklessly, for the pleasure of an eager audience; that, notwithstanding his lexicon of trademark licks and transitions, he never repeated himself; that he was witty, irreverent, and unpredictable; that he could play any piece in any key; that though his virtuousity may occasionally have been impaired by stimulants, it never withered into glibness; that every solo was a direct expression of the moment in which it was played; and that the source of his inspiration was unfettered. It abided almost until the end.

Consider one example among many, "All the Things You Are," by Jerome Kern and Oscar Hammerstein II, written in 1939 for the stage show, *Very Warm For May*. Its substitute chords and key changes appealed to the modernists, and Gillespie turned it into a bop theme at a 1945 session with Parker, who played only the eight-bar release. The introductory vamp they fashioned is still standard in jazz versions of the tune. Parker performed the song often with his own quintet, and in his years with Chan affectionately called it "Yatag," an anagram of his favorite phrase from the lyric, "You are the angel glow." When, in 1947, he recorded it for

(Left to right) Tommy Potter, Charlie Parker, Dizzy Gillespie, John Coltrane at Birdland, New York City, 1951.

Dial, three takes were made, on all of which the vamp was dramatized as a kind of surrogate theme. On the first take, Parker plays Kern's melody with embellishments, departing from it only toward the end of his chorus. On the second, he improvises freely at once (justifying a title change to "Bird of Paradise"). On the third (master take), he improvises a startlingly original variation that owes nothing to Kern's melody and which, despite his waggish reference to Chopin right before the release, has the integrity of deliberated composition. His later performances of the song include those from Sweden in late 1950 and from the celebrated concert at Massey Hall, Toronto, in 1953. Yet perhaps the most remarkable version was hidden for twenty-seven years, as it was recorded at a jam session in 1950, where Parker, the honored guest, regaled a group of white acolytes. Released on an album called *Apartment Sessions*, it alone finds Parker playing the piece capaciously (a four-chorus solo spliced to a two-chorus solo), as he combines embellishment and improvisation for an extraordinarily intricate invention.

Below: (left to right) Bud Powell, Charles Mingus, Max Roach, Dizzy Gillespie, Charlie Parker, at Massey Hall, Toronto, May 1953.

Opposite page: (left to right) Charles Mingus, Thelonious Monk, Roy Haynes, Charlie Parker, at the Open Door, New York City, January 1953.

(Left to right) Charlie Parker, Ross Russell, Harold West, Earl Coleman, Shifty Henry, at a Dial Records session, Los Angeles, February 1947.

The years 1947–48 seem almost a period of grace, or at least a respite from overt turbulence. He attempted a stable home life with Doris, who had traveled to Camarillo and visited him there daily. Chan had also flown to California, but she was pregnant by another man and left when Bird asked her to abort. When he was finally released into Doris's care, he seemed optimistic. Although furious with Ross Russell for releasing "Lover Man," an inforgivable wound to his vanity, Bird recorded two sessions for him in L.A.: the first was a blues and ballads affair with Erroll Garner and a singer he encouraged, Earl Coleman; the second (with McGhee and Wardell Gray) amounted to a health report conveyed in song titles: "Relaxin' At Camarillo," "Cheers," "Stupendous," and the first of his two contrapuntal themes, "Carvin' the Bird." (The second was "Ah-Leu-Cha" in 1948.) Once resettled in New York, he organized the most steadfast of his bands, with Miles, Max, Duke Jordan or Al Haig, and Tommy Potter, for long residencies at the Royal Roost and the Three Deuces. With Billy Shaw managing him, he embarked on successful visits to Chicago, Detroit, Philadelphia, Washington, D.C., and elsewhere. Critics continued to snipe at him (Leonard Feather and Barry Ulanov were notable exceptions) and salaries were at best fair. But his fame among musicians was absolute and his ever-growing coterie was enthusiastic to the point of worship. At a 1948 concert with Gillespie's big band at Chicago's Pershing Ballroom (taped but never released), his scrupulously paced alto elicits congregational responses from the audience of three thousand, as though he were preaching a sermon to reverent followers.

He tried to free himself from narcotics and did not submit easily to the baseness of a life ordained by addiction. Gerry Mulligan believes he hated having to ask for handouts and masked his mortification with arrogance, as though he were demanding his rightful due, donations to underwrite his genius. As dozens of younger musicians would soon learn, heroin was a sedative that relieved the stimulation of staying up all night every night—a requisite of the jazz life that wasn't necessarily in tune with each musician's metabolism. It grieved Parker to see musicians imitating him, and he told them as well as interviewers that he played best straight, that he wished they would do as he said and not as he did, that he'd been hooked since the age of twelve and therefore could not help himself. He provided a more graphic lesson to Mulligan, who occasionally stayed with Bird at his 140th Street apartment. "He kept drugs away from me, but after we'd spent a lot of time together, he injected himself in my presence and said, 'This is something that I have to do. It's terrible but I'm stuck with it.' It was terrifying to watch my hero doing that. He made it as revolting as possible, as though it were a lecture on what not to do." In attempting to substitute alcohol for drugs, Bird gave himself a bleeding ulcer. Still, omnipresent pushers thwarted him with powdery packets surreptitiously dropped in his coat pockets.

One striking aspect of Parker's addiction is that it never entirely subverted his personality. He remained dignified, open, generous, curious, concerned. His pleasure in encouraging young musicians, in sharing his comprehensive fund of information, is a commonplace in the recollections of those who knew him. Few musicians, if any, understood the hellishness of heroin in the 1940s, but all addicts quickly learned—and many were attracted by—the intricacies of copping, a time-consuming occupation that structured their lives. Given the energies Bird expended on his habit it is all the more remarkable that he managed to sustain constancy in his music, hold the loyalties of an increasing band of grateful disciples, and wear all the masks necessitated by a daily circuit that involved furtive connections, middle-class propriety, and bravura inspiration. Conversely, it is no surprise at all that he wore himself out at thirty-four.

The assuagement of any addiction is private, morbid, and dull. Only the evidence of personality vanquishing obsession can interest posterity. Never noted for stability or punctuality, Parker's professional behavior eventually became so erratic that club

Top: John Lewis with Dizzy Gillespie Orchestra, at the Savoy Ballroom, New York City, 1946.
Bottom: Unknown, Billie Holiday, Charlie Parker.

Top: Charlie Parker in back of the Apollo Theatre, 126th Street, New York City, August 17, 1950, eating lobster.

Bottom: Gerry Mulligan and Zoot Sims, 126th Street, New York City, August 17, 1950.

Opposite page: Charlie Parker at the Open Door, New York City, January 1953.

. . . .

owners would book him for single evenings, sometimes single sets. But nothing enfeebled his devotion to the community of musicians or his passion for increasing his knowledge of music. Mulligan's example is instructive. They met in Philadelphia when Parker and Gillespie were set to play a concert opposite the Elliot Lawrence radio orchestra, for which Mulligan was an arranger. Only nineteen, he knew Parker's recordings with Red Norvo. ("Imagine what it did to a young kid to hear Bird play on that blues. His clean, precise statements shone like gems.") On the day of the concert, Mulligan was asked to fill in on tenor when a member of the band broke his writst. Bird came to the rehearsal and "was lovely and charming and gracious to the band and Elliot. He was complimentary about the music and about my charts." He invited everyone to the Downbeat Club for a post-concert jam sesison. Mulligan arrived at the club, checked the tenor in the coat room, and listened to two sets of Bird, Diz, and Don Byas. "Can you see me playing with them? Don Byas would have cut me five new belly buttons." He told Bird how much he enjoyed it and prepared to leave. "What do you mean?" Bird said. "Wait a minute." He strode to the coat room, retrieved the tenor, put it together, blew a scale, handed it to Mulligan, and insisted he play. "He had such dignity about him and command. His way of speaking was so correct, with none of the jive we associate with musicians."

Roland Hanna was another beneficiary, whose first experience with Bird "was like a revelation." Bird and Al Haig were late for the set at the Paradise Ballroom in Detroit, and Hanna was asked to fill in. He sat down at the piano and played "How High the Moon." "All of a sudden this great wind passed through my ears and I looked around and it was Charlie Parker. Hearing his first few notes I got so small I felt I was in the eye of a hurricane, but he told me to continue." On another occasion in Detroit some of the local musicians—Hanna, Barry Harris, Tommy Flanagan, Hugh Lawson, Doug Watkins—went to see him, and he spent his entire intermission period talking to them about "bass lines and chords and the whole idea of orchestration. It was a tremendous teaching experience. He didn't keep anything to himself. He felt that the information he had everyone should have, and he sat with us from the matinee to the show that night at eight."

As generous as Bird was to young hopefuls,* he could express

*One of the most vivid portraits of Bird befriending a young fan is found in Chapter 4 of David Amram's autobiography, *Vibrations*, It brings together an uncanny number of standard elements in Parker anecdotes. A twenty-two-year-old student, musician, composer, and gym teacher, dangling in anticipation of the draft, Amram talks, jams, and parties with Bird, who teaches him about Delius and demonstrates telepathic powers concerning the presence of cops.

The Metronome All Stars at RCA Studios, New York City, 1949.

his displeasure with caustic economy. Muhal Richard Abrams heard him at the Bee Hive in Chicago on a night when Bird was having trouble with the local rhythm section. He walked over to each of the three musicians, with one finger raised to his lips and the other hand motioning to them to desist playing. When all was quiet, he resumed and completed the set unaccompanied. He knew how to handle cocky players. Buddy De Franco recalls a young tenor who challenged Bird on "All the Things You Are." Parker welcomed him to the stand, counted off the number, and played in a key that nobody played. "The kid was devastated, and Bird could do that to anybody. He taught me that trick of playing in all the keys, because it forces you away from your basic patterns—from what we call fail-safe jazz." He was intent on getting his friends to listen to everything, high and low. He told David Amram, "If you want to understand my music, listen to the Clovers." When the sculptress Julie Macdonald referred to an "unctuous sounding" saxophonist who appeared with him, he smiled and said, "Oh, his sound is a good contrast to mine, a perfect foil for me."

Conversation with De Franco often turned to Prokofiev, since Bird knew Prokofiev was his favorite composer:

Everytime he'd get a new recording of Prokofiev, he'd say let's go to my place and listen. He knew about so many things. We were in New York in the winter, working some concert together, and we'd been up all night. It was snowing, freezing cold, and I wanted to get back to the hotel and sleep, but we passed the Salvation Army Band, and he says, 'Wait a minute, let me hear this.' I can't believe this is Charlie Parker standing in the snow listening to this horrible band—I missed whatever cues he found in there. Finally I said, 'OK, I'll catch you later.' It wasn't until next spring that I got a job on Fifty-second Street. He was playing at another club and I'd go down during my breaks to hear him. The first time I walked in I sat very close to the stage, he gave me a little nod, pointed his sax at me, and played one of those pieces from the Salvation Army."

De Franco saw another side of Bird when they finished a gig in Providence and visited a friend of the clarinetist. Talking and drinking, they missed the last train to the city. Just before daylight, a couple of neighbors came by. They'd been hunting for four days and had a slew of rabbits they didn't know how to dress. Bird said, "Wait a minute, I know how to dress them." He put on an apron, took the rabbits down to the cellar, and cleaned and fixed them all.

Parker imparted a telling lesson about overwriting to John Lewis at Miles Davis's 1947 Savoy session. Bred in Albuquerque,

(Left to right) Tommy Potter, Charlie Parker, Max Roach, Miles Davis, Duke Jordan, at the Three Deuces, New York City, 1948.

(Left to right) Buddy Rich, Ray Brown, Charlie Parker, Max Hollander, Mitch Miller, unknown, at Mercury Records session, first date with strings ("Just Friends"), November 30, 1949.

· · · · · · · · · · ·

(Left to right) Hot Lips Page, Tommy Potter, unknown, Big Chief Russell Moore, Sidney Bechet, Al Haig, Charlie Parker, Max Roach, Miles Davis, Kenny Dorham, arriving in France, 1949.

Lewis recognized the purity and clean melodicism of Parker's conception as an outgrowth of the southwestern style. It was less self-conscious than the New York approach to progressive harmonies. Yet Lewis was himself given to laboring a score. To celebrate his friendship with Miles, he made him the gift of a new piece called "Milestones." At rehearsal, Bird, who played tenor on the date, told him, "John, I can't play this—too many changes going by too fast. I'll just play the bridge," which is what he did. Lewis was the pianist five weeks later at a Dizzy Gillespie concert at Carnegie Hall; Parker was added at the last minute, without benefit of rehearsal. "Everyone was too excited, the tempos ran away." Yet Parker's lusty attack was beguiling, blinding—as the bootleg recordings made clear. Dizzy told Lewis, "If I had the money I'd take care of Yard permanently. I'd build him a home and take care of him."

His home life fluctuated, his personal tempo quickened just as he began to achieve worldwide recognition among musicians. Bird's first visit abroad in 1949 was a confirmation as well as a success. He attended a concert by Segovia which exemplified his belief that an artist should be able to hold an audience without theatrics. His own concerts brought home the realization that in Paris he could receive the kind of respect reserved for classical recitalists at home. When he returned he took Doris to Detroit and visited Rebecca, who had graduated from Dress Design School, and her husband and Leon. He looked slender and healthy, and came bearing gifts: an alto sax for Leon, and for Rebecca perfume and the album he'd recorded with strings. Later, she realized that in bringing her that particular album, Charlie was making a pun: his nickname for her, Rebec, is also the name for the bowed string instruments that predate the violin (from the Latin *ribeca*). That evening he made another gesture. Performing at the Mirror Ballroom, he dedicated "Body and Soul," the song that undid him at his first Kansas City jam session, to "my first love and the mother of my son," and "April in Paris" to her husband.

Before summer's end, he broke off with Doris and moved in with Chan on the Lower East Side. He adopted her daughter Kim as his own and had two more children with Chan, Pree, a daughter, and a son Baird. The only one of his wives, licensed or common-law, who called him Bird instead of Charlie, Chan was a fan who also recognized Bird's desire for bourgeois stolidity. To her his life "was a joyous thing—he lived his life fully, loved his kids, music, movies—westerns, shoot-em-ups. Simple things, Bird liked simple things. He was the strongest man I ever met in my life." Their brownstone was in a neighborhood famed for its ethnic mix, and Bird occasionally invited musicians over to hear the exotic musics, though his catholic tastes took a more popular turn at home. When he wasn't listening to modern classics, he played a few

Above: Paris Jazz Festival audience, Pleyel, Paris, 1949.
Below: Charlie and Chan Parker, c. 1951.

current hits repeatedly, singing along in stentorian tones—Kay Kyser's "On a Slow Boat to China" (a song he performed several times at the Roost), Mario Lanza's "Be My Love," Peggy Lee's "Lover Man." Leonard Feather suggests that part of Bird longed to be a square, and Phil Woods, whom Chan married years later, agrees that when Bird and Chan took a place in New Hope, he "played the role, commuting to Trenton with his newspaper."

Yet Bird was not one for solitude, and the shorter commute from the East Side must have seemed more natural, fulfilling his need for people, music, and other stimulants. One night at the Roost he gushingly described a new Stravinsky record to drummer Ed Shaughnessy. The next night he told him, "Eddie, you've got to come up to this Rumanian restaurant with me. They have this fantastic folk group with some authentic stringed instruments and percussion, and you know something, they swing more than we do!" On a beautiful May afternoon he ran into Al Cohn at the Turf Restaurant on Forty-ninth Street, and invited him home:

He even paid for the cab, which was quite an honor—being treated by Bird. They had a very nice place. After a while, he told Chan we were going out to have a few drinks. It was a Ukrainian neighborhood and we went to three or four different bars. All the Ukrainians, working-class guys, knew him as Charlie. I don't think they knew he was a musician, but it was obvious they liked him and were glad to see him. I saw a different side of him: he was like a middle-class guy with middle-class values."

Chan recalls his hurt at the lack of recognition—articles about modern jazz that ignored him or treated his music as a by-product of hipster jive and frantic hype. Yet his influence was becoming ubiquitous. In 1950, the city's largest jazz club, on Fifty-second Street and Broadway, was renamed in his honor: Birdland, "the jazz corner of the world." He owned no part of it, of course, and within a few years was banned from the place. Bird made at least three appearances on television, of which only one has survived. Norman Granz, the producer of JATP and most of Bird's later records, arranged to make a film of him, but the sound track was lost. Older musicians, stars, began to echo his ideas. Benny Goodman, who called him "certainly one of the most brilliant men in the whole field of jazz music," made a couple of bop records, including one based on "Stealin' Apples," the song that had inspired Charlie back on Olive Street. *Down Beat* ran an odd letter from a soldier in Korea who took a Parker record "off a Chinese Communist" he'd killed. "He must have been a hip fel-

Top: Aimé Barelli, Charlie Parker, backstage at the Paris Jazz Festival, Pleyel, Paris, 1949.
Bottom: Charlie Parker, Big Chief Russell Moore, Pleyel, Paris, 1949.
Opposite page: Charlie Parker and Max Roach at the train station at Marseilles, 1949.

Top: (Left to right) Charlie Parker, Billy Strayhorn,
Roy Eldridge, Sweden, 1950.
Bottom: Edgard Varèse

low to have a carefully wrapped recording of Parker's 'Bird of
Paradise.' It hurt me pretty bad to remember how he clutched the
record in his hands."

In November Bird was back in Europe, including a week in
Sweden, though his addiction was now more debilitating than
ever. Joe Newman says he was insufficiently paid in Stockholm
and spent all his money on fixes. A Swedish musician remembers a drive through farm country in a car full of musicians, one
of whom told Bird that cows love music. Bird asked the driver to
pull over. He assembled his horn, walked into the field, bowed
formally to a cow as though requesting the next dance, and gave
her a taste of modern jazz. His own tastes were changing. The
passion for classicism and his regrets at never having studied
theory soured into frustration. He was tired of blues and pop-song
forms; they had been his musical gravity and he now felt con-
strained by them. He hoped to commission a work by Stefan
Wolpe and implored Edgard Varèse to take him as a student.
Varèse told Reisner of Parker's visits: "He'd come in and ex-
claim, 'Take me as you would a baby and teach me music. I only
write in one voice. I want to have structure. I want to write orchestra scores. . . .' He spoke of being tired of the environment his
works relegated him to. 'I'm so steeped in this and can't get out.'"

Although he persuaded Norman Granz to help him launch an
ensemble of strings, with which he toured and recorded ("Just
Friends" was his best-selling record), the initial arrangements
were by dance-band hacks and made little use of the modern ideas
he relished. Had he lived, that would have undoubtedly changed.
He asked Jimmy Mundy to write a new arrangement of "Easy to
Love," and gratefully accepted a theme for strings by George

Russell and a couple of challenging pieces by Mulligan. A chance to perform them all came in 1952, when he was hired for a dance at Harlem's Rockland Palace, a memorable evening. The event was a benefit for Benjamin Davis, an attorney and city council member, who was the last Communist to hold elected office in the United States. In a trial that flagrantly violated due process, Davis was sentenced to five years for advocating the violent overthrow of the country. The case became a cause célèbre on the left. Bird played four or five sets that night, with his quintet as well as the strings, and he was robust. The prospect of leading his ensemble before thousands of dancers had greater appeal then the political solemnity of the occasion, which by no means dampened his ir-

Charlie Parker and strings.

Charlie and Chan Parker.

reverent wit. When Paul Robeson sang "Water Boy," Bird trotted to the stage with a glass of water. Chan brought along the tape recorder Bird had bought her as a birthday present and preserved much of the evening's music, which was exceptional.* Though the apex is an extended, rapid-fire solo on "Lester Leaps In," accompanied by the miraculously reactive Max Roach, the performances with the strings embody the tension between banal formulas and blues-based visions. Highlights include a rare version of "Star Dust" and the Mulligan originals, "Goldrush" and "Rocker." It was one of Parker's last grand nights.

Mulligan introduced Bird to his psychologist, who agreed to see him for sessions in his car. The doctor, though bound by confidentiality, readily admits he thought Bird "wonderful," and was amused when Bird told him that he'd only get paid if he came down to the club where he was working and had a drink with him, which he did. Yet a series of crushing events ensued, and the final descent took on vertiginous speed. Although never arrested on a narcotics charge (a seeming miracle that prompted an unsubstantiated rumor that he collaborated with the police), Bird's cabaret license was arbitrarily revoked for nearly two years. During

*Someone else taped the evening as well and released several albums, which don't include "Star Dust," "Goldrush," or George Russell's theme. Nor is the sound as vivid as Chan's. Her tapes were bought by Columbia Records in 1980, but never released.

that time, he couldn't work in a New York jazz club. Suffering severely from bleeding ulcers, humiliated by promoters who would no longer hire him because of various disputes that he took to the union for arbitration, seized by exhaustion and depression, Parker began to crumble. That he could summon forth strength and radiance until nearly the end is borne out by tapes that document his playing through the end of 1954. But there were other nights when admirers turned away in embarrassment. An album of Cole Porter songs was disastrous. When he was featured in *Ebony* as the patriarch of a happy, integrated family, dining with Chan and Kim on a meal prepared as a photographer's prop, Rebecca and her husband filed charges for nonsupport of Leon. Admitting he hadn't paid any money in fourteen years, Bird was jailed in Detroit until he came up with $350, 10 percent of the debt. Early in 1954, King Pleasure's vocalized version of "Parker's Mood," one of Bird's consummate blues performances, was issued. The lyric prophesied his imminent death and concluded: "Don't cry for me/ 'Cause I'm going to Kansas City." A nonplussed Parker told Chan, "Don't let them bury me in Kansas City." On March 7, 1954, while visiting Julie Macdonald in California, he learned that his daughter Pree, not yet three, had died of a congenital heart condition. He broke.

Top: (left to right) Rebecca, Rebecca's husband, Ross, Teddy Blume, Charlie Parker, Leon Parker.
Bottom: Baird and Charlie Parker, Washington Square Park, New York City.

The details of Parker's final months have been rehearsed endlessly. Many witnesses have told how he and the strings were booked into Birdland as soon as his cabaret card was returned, and an argument ensued that ended with Bird getting fired, going home, and—after an altercation with Chan—swallowing iodine; how he was twice hospitalized in Bellevue; how his relationship with Chan deteriorated and they separated near the close of 1954;* how during the rootless months in the West Village, his consumption of cheap wine exacerbated his ulcer, which prevented him from getting much sleep. Mulligan went to hear him for the last time in mid-1954: "He was faltering. I cried. His playing had exuberance at best, at worst a manic velocity, but always a musical control. What was missing was the kind of gentleness he could project." Buddy Tate ran into him on the street after he'd finished playing in the backup band on a pop singer's record date and bought him a drink. When Tate told him about the recording session, Bird asked him why they never called him for gigs like that. "Bird, everybody probably thinks your price is too high." "Oh man, I'd love to do those things." He sometimes played in joints that were little more than storefronts, usually with minor musicians. During intermission at a Village bar that later became the

*Before the breakup he made a separate peace with Rebecca, when they visited her in Detroit, and he cryptically apologized.

(Left to right) Benny Carter, Barney Kessell, Flip Phillips, Charlie Shavers, Ray Brown, Charlie Parker, Oscar Peterson, J.C. Heard, Ben Webster, Johnny Hodges, at a Clef recording session, Hollywood, California, July 1952.

. . . .

Charlie Parker at the Bee Hive in Chicago two weeks
before his death, 1955.

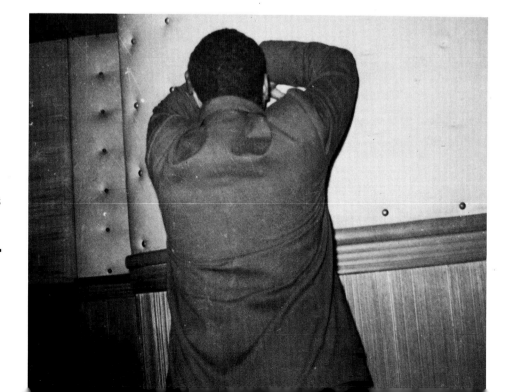

Cafe Bohemia, Ahmed Basheer, with whom he was living, and Nat Lorber, a trumpet player known as Face, stood outside smoking a joint. Bird joined them and said, "Let's all go down to the Brooklyn Bridge, hold hands, and jump off."

One night Bird made a panicky late-night visit to the 103rd Street apartment of a woman who had managed him, Maely Daniele, a Czechoslovakian-born jazz enthusiast formerly married to the actor Freddie Bartholomew, who was keeping company with William Dufty, a reporter for *The New York Post* and her future husband. They awoke to a slamming in the inner doorway, and Dufty feared it might be trouble relating to a story he was covering, until the concierge called up, "It's only Parker." He wrapped himself in a towel and opened the door:

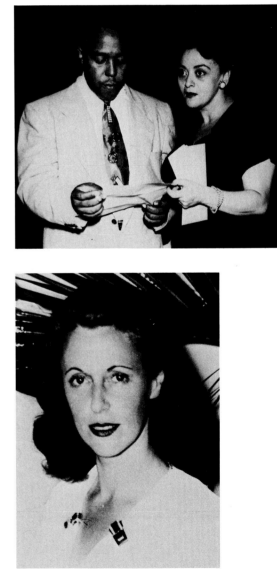

Top: Charlie Parker and Maely Dufty, c. 1952. Bottom: Baroness Pannonica "Nica" de Koenigswarter.

It was a typical midnight visitation when someone comes by to unburden himself. Charlie's conversation was infra dig about being strung out, looking for drugs or money. He spoke of Moishe Levy and Oscar Goodstein, the Birdland heavies. He talked about poems he wrote and made a joke about visiting people late at night and reciting a poem. He said that the females who were smart enough to keep the poems realized their value. His language was succinct and distilled—things he'd brooded over and reduced to rhythmic, comic word-riffs. As a writer, I was very impressed. During that time he was gigging for a few bucks a night with pickup bands at various joints, no publicity. He was fat and in very bad shape. Christ on the cross is not an image I carry with me, but the image of that man's face—it seemed to be bleeding, you just wanted to apply a tourniquet. He recapped the business about the child Pree. What could you do? You didn't have the drugs or the money. You listened."

There was a final confrontation at Birdland, a bandstand fight between Parker and Bud Powell. Days later he was set to play at Storyville in Boston. He never made the trip. Instead he dropped by the Stanhope Hotel, on March 9, to visit Baroness Pannonica de Koenigswarter, a wealthy jazz enthusiast who befriended musicians and successfully flouted racist conventions. She knew how sick he was when he refused a drink. A doctor was called, but no attempt was made to move him; none of his friends was notified. He phoned Addie in Kansas City, who told him not to go to hospital, that he would die there, that he should come to her. On March 12, a Saturday night, he died while watching jugglers on the Tommy Dorsey show. "At the moment of his going, there was a tremendous clap of thunder," the baroness later said. An autopsy attributed cause of death to lobar pneumonia. For reasons never adequately explained, the body arrived at Bellevue more than five hours after he died, marked John Parker, age fifty-three. Two days later, the baroness held a late-night press conference and explained that she had decided not to report his death until she could locate Chan.

But word was already out. Gene Ramey told Doris, who called Addie. Moreover, the scrawled legend, "Bird Lives!" began appearing on Greenwich Village walls that weekend. If his death was little noted in the newspapers, the gossip rags plummeted to a level of scurrility that makes contemporary journalism seem relatively pristine. The fact that a black musician died in the home of a wealthy, titled white woman was of far more interest than his music. The farce that followed, as Doris and Chan fought over the body, causing its removal from one funeral parlor to another, and ending with a Kansas City burial complete with a tombstone engraved with the wrong date, added more fuel to the scandal, as did the endless court battle over his estate.

As Auden wrote of Yeats, Parker's gift survived it all: "The parish of rich women, physical decay, yourself." He triumphed over contempt, neglect, and mindless worship; over the nexus of commercial interests that sought to market his music as passing jive. His life and personality are subjects of great passion; his women especially are caught in the play, each championing her own gospel. In many respects, the music also remains a private passion. Despite its incalculable influence, the specific legacy of Parker's genius is known to a small but worldwide cult. Admirers wonder at the absence of civil honors (statues, streets, parks, stamps), though a more acute absence is that of adequate recognition in studies that purport to evaluate "serious" music. While the philistines guard the gates of culture, the immediacy of Parker's achievement continues to astonish. You hear him, perhaps unexpectedly, when you walk into a friend's house, or on the car radio, or worked into a film score, and you are struck by the relentless energy, the uncorrupted humanity of his music. It is never without direction. This most restive, capricious of men is unequivocal in his art. He never deigns merely to impress, to blind with virtuoso dazzle. He draws you in, raises you up. His ballads are stirringly candid, his fiery free flights filled with zeal, desire, rage, love. Was he more enthralled by life or terrified by it? Dead at thirty-four, played out like a bad song, looking twenty years his senior. Yet Bird lives. Bird is the truth. Bird is love. Bird is thousands of musical fragments, each a direct expression of a time and place—the mosaic burst into radiant bits. As with Mozart, the facts of Charlie Parker's life make little sense because they fail to explain his music. Perhaps his life is what his music overcame. And overcomes.

Charlie Parker's wrongly dated gravestone, Lincoln Cemetery, Kansas City, Missouri.

Opposite page: Charlie Parker, publicity photograph, mid-1940s.

A Selected Discography
of Long-Playing Records

MANY SESSIONS are available, whole or in part, on competing labels; I've chosen editions that, taken together, duplicate as little material as possible. Of the numerous Parker tapes that remain unissued, I've included two (marked with asterisks) that are expected to be released soon and are of unusual historical importance. Each listing begins with the title of the album and the catalog number, followed by a few principal musicians who play on it (those in parentheses appear without Parker). Also appended is information regarding recording locations (states, countries), dates, and circumstances, i.e., whether the music was recorded in the studio; through radio or television broadcast facilities; or privately. The entries for each of Parker's three prominent label affiliations (Savoy, Dial, Verve) begin with inclusive editions, followed by well-known anthologies culled from the complete works.

THE APPRENTICE YEARS/SIDEMAN RECORDINGS

• "Honeysuckle Rose/Body and Soul." Unaccompanied. Missouri; c. 1937–39; private.*

• *First Recordings!* (Xanadu ORI 221). With Jay McShann and His Orchestra, Clyde Hart's All Stars, the Cootie Williams Sextet. Kansas, New York; 1940–45; broadcast, private, studio.

• *Jay McShann: The Early Bird* (MCA 1338). With McShann's Orchestra (and quartet). Texas, Illinois, New York; 1941–42; studio.

• *Birth of the Bebop* (Stash ST 260). With Dizzy Gillespie, Oscar Pettiford, Don Byas, Miles Davis, Roy Haynes, the Chet Baker Quartet. Illinois, New York, California; 1943–53; private.

• *Dizzy Gillespie: In the Beginning* (Prestige 24030). Two discs with the Dizzy Gillespie Sextet, Quintet (big band, and other bands). New York; 1945; studio.

• *Every Bit of It/Charlie Parker 1945* (Spotlite SPJ-150D). Two discs with Clyde Hart's All Stars, Cootie Williams Sextet and Orchestra (no Parker solos), Sarah Vaughan, Sir Charles Thompson and His All Stars, Slim Gaillard and His Orchestra. New York, California; 1945; studio, broadcast.

• *Red Norvo: Fabulous Jam Session* (Spotlite 127). With Norvo, Dizzy Gillespie, Teddy Wilson, Flip Phillips, Slam Stewart, Specs Powell. New York; 1945; studio.

• *Miles Davis: Collector's Items* (Prestige 7044). With Davis, Sonny Rollins, Walter Bishop, Percy Heath, Philly Joe Jones. New York; 1953; studio.

THE SAVOYS

The complete Savoy studio recordings consist of thirty master takes and seventy-six false starts and alternate takes. Except for a few scraps of "Marma-duke," they are collected in a boxed set of five discs.

- *The Complete Savoy Studio Sessions* (Savoy SJ5 5500). Five discs with the Tiny Grimes Quintet, the Miles Davis All Stars, Dizzy Gillespie, Bud Powell, John Lewis, Duke Jordan, Sadik Hakim, Curly Russell, Tommy Potter, Max Roach. New York, Detroit; 1944–48; studio.
- *Bird/The Savoy Recordings (Master Takes)* (Savoy SJL 2201). Two discs, thirty master takes.
- *Encores* (Savoy SJL 1107). Sixteen alternate takes.
- *Encores Vol. 2* (Savoy SJL 1129). Fifteen alternate takes, including four false starts on "Marmaduke" inadvertently omitted from the "complete" edition.

THE DIALS

As issued by Spotlite, Warners, and Stateside, the most complete editions of the Dial recordings consist of thirty-five master takes, forty-eight alternate takes, three home recordings, and an alternate from Red Norvo's Dial session (see Spotlite 127 above). They are collected on six discs, singly or boxed.

- *Charlie Parker on Dial, Vol. 1* (Spotlite 101). With Miles Davis, Lucky Thompson, Dodo Marmarosa, Arv Garrison, Dizzy Gillespie, Howard McGhee. California; 1946; studio.
- *Charlie Parker on Dial, Vol. 2* (Spotlite 102). With Erroll Garner, Earl Coleman, Red Callender, Doc West. California; 1947; studio.
- *Charlie Parker on Dial, Vol. 3* (Spotlite 103). With Howard McGhee, Wardell Gray, Dodo Marmarosa, Barney Kessel, Russ Freeman. California; 1947; studio, private.
- *Charlie Parker on Dial, Vol. 4* (Spotlite 104). With Miles Davis, Duke Jordan, Tommy Potter, Max Roach. New York; 1947; studio.
- *Charlie Parker on Dial, Vol. 5* (Spotlite 105). With Miles Davis, Duke Jordan, Tommy Potter, Max Roach, Red Norvo, Lucky Thompson, Earl Coleman. New York, California; 1945–47; studio.
- *Charlie Parker on Dial, Vol. 6* (Spotlite 106). With Miles Davis, J. J. Johnson, Duke Jordan, Tommy Potter, Max Roach. New York; 1947; studio.
- *Bird Symbols* (Charlie Parker 407). Twelve master takes.
- *The Very Best of Bird* (Warner Bros. 3198). Two discs, twenty-six selections—seven alternates were mistakenly substituted for the master takes.

THE VERVES

The complete Verves consist of eighty-seven master takes and seventeen alternates, in addition to eleven concert performances with Jazz at the Philharmonic and four "jam session" vehicles by an all-star studio band. They are collected in a boxed set of ten discs.

- *Charlie Parker on Verve* (Verve 00MJ 3268/77). Ten discs with Jazz at the Philharmonic, Neal Hefti, Machito, Kenny Dorham, Red Rodney, Dizzy Gillespie, Miles Davis, Ben Webster, Johnny Hodges, Benny Carter, Benny Harris, Al Haig, Hank Jones, Thelonious Monk, Walter Bishop, Jr., John Lewis, Oscar Peterson, Tommy Potter, Ray Brown, Teddy Kotick, Max Roach, Buddy Rich, Roy Haynes, Kenny Clarke; big band, strings. California, New York; 1946–54; studio, concert.
- *Night and Day/The Genius of Charlie Parker, Vol. 1* (Verve 8003). Twelve master takes with big band and strings.
- *April in Paris/The Genius of Charlie Parker, Vol. 2* (Verve 8004). Twelve master takes with strings.

- *Now's the Time/The Genius of Charlie Parker, Vol. 3* (Verve 8005). Eight master takes and four alternates with quartet.
- *Bird and Diz/The Genius of Charlie Parker, Vol. 4* (Verve 8006). Six master takes and five alternates with quintet.
- *Cole Porter/The Genius of Charlie Parker, Vol. 5* (Verve 8007). Six master takes and three alternates with quintet.
- *Fiesta/The Genius of Charlie Parker, Vol. 6* (Verve 8008). Ten master takes and two alternates with quintet, sextet.
- *Jazz Perennial/The Genius of Charlie Parker, Vol. 7* (Verve [J] MV-2617). Nineteen master takes with various groups.
- *Swedish Schnapps/The Genius of Charlie Parker, Vol. 8* (Verve 8010). Nine master takes and four alternates with quintet.

- *The Cole Porter Songbook* (Verve 823 250-1). Eleven master takes with quintet, strings, big band.
- *The Verve Years (1948–50)* (Verve VE2-2501). Two discs, twenty-one master takes and one alternate with various groups.
- *The Verve Years (1950–51)* (Verve VE2-2512). Two discs, twenty-nine master takes with various groups.
- *The Verve Years (1952–1954)* (Verve VE2-2523). Two discs, thirty master takes with various groups.
- *Jazz at the Philharmonic/Bird and Pres: Carnegie Hall 1949* (Verve 815 150 1). Four selections with JATP.
- *Norman Granz Jam Session* (Verve VE2-2508). Two discs, four selections with all-star ensemble.
- *Afro-Cuban Jazz* (Verve VE2-2522). Two discs, eleven selections with Machito (others without Parker).

BROADCASTS/CONCERTS/PRIVATE RECORDINGS

With a couple of exceptions, the following records—some of them slovenly edited and packaged "bootleg" albums—are listed in chronological order according to the earliest performance in the package. The exceptions are those in which only one selection is from an earlier year than the bulk of the album's music.

- *Yardbird in Lotus Land* (Spotlite SPJ 123). With Dizzy Gillespie and His Rebop Six, Miles Davis, Joe Albany, Nat Cole, Buddy Rich. California; 1945–46; private, broadcast.
- *Lullaby in Rhythm* (Spotlite SPJ 107). With Barry Ulanov's All Star Modern Jazz Musicians, Howard McGhee Quintet. California, New York; 1947; private, broacast.
- *It Happened One Night* (Natural Organic 7000). With Dizzy Gillespie, John Lewis, Al McKibbon, Joe Harris (Ella Fitzgerald). New York; 1947; private.
- *Anthropology* (Spotlite SPJ 108). With Barry Ulanov and His All Star Metronome Jazzmen (Sarah Vaughan, Tadd Dameron). New York; 1948; broadcast.
- *Bird on 52nd Street* (Jazz Workshop JWS 501). With Duke Jordan, Tommy Potter, Max Roach, Miles Davis. New York; 1948; private.

- Charlie Parker with Dizzy Gillespie and His Orchestra at the Pershing Ballroom. Illinois; 1948; private.*
- *The Complete Royal Roost Performances, Vol. One* (Savoy SJL 2259). With Miles Davis, Kenny Dorham, Tadd Dameron, Al Haig, Curly Russell, Tommy Potter, Max Roach. New York; 1948–49; broadcast.
- *The Complete Royal Roost Performances, Vol. Two* (Savoy SJL 2260). With Kenny Dorham, Lucky Thompson, Milt Jackson, Al Haig, Tommy Potter, Max Roach, Joe Harris. New York; 1949; broadcast.
- *Bird on the Road* (Jazz Showcase 5003). With Kenny Dorham, Lucky Thompson, Brew Moore, Milt Jackson, Al Haig. New York, Montreal; 1949–53; private, broadcast.
- *Bird in Paris* (Spotlite SPJ 118). With Kenny Dorham, Al Haig, Tommy Potter, Max Roach, Maurice Moufflard. Paris; 1949–50; private, broadcast.

- *1949 Unissued Performances by Charlie Parker* (Jazz Live BLJ 8004). With Red Rodney, Al Haig, Tommy Potter, Max Roach. New York; 1949; broadcast.
- *Bird at St. Nick's* (Jazz Workshop JSW 500). With Al Haig, Tommy Potter, Roy Haynes, Red Rodney. New York; 1950; private.
- *Rappin' with Bird* (Meexa Discox). With a twenty-minute interview of Parker by Marshall Stearns and John Maher, plus his quintet, strings. New York, California; 1946–50; private, broadcast.
- *Apartment Sessions* (Spotlite SPJ 146). With John Williams, Phil Brown, Frank Isola. New York; 1950; private.
- *One Night in Birdland* (Columbia JG-34808). Two discs with Fats Navarro, Bud Powell, Curly Russell, Art Blakey. New York; 1950; broadcast.
- *Bird at the Apollo* (Charlie Parker CP-503). With strings, Al Haig, Roy Haynes, Sarah Vaughan (Stan Getz, Timmy Rogers). New York; 1950; private.
- *At the Pershing Ballroom* (Zim ZM-1003). With Chris Anderson, George Freeman, Bruz Freeman. Illinois; 1950; private.
- *One Night in Chicago* (Savoy SJL 1132). With Claude McLin, Chris Anderson, George Freeman. Illinois; 1950; private.
- *Bird in Sweden* (Spotlite SPJ 124-5). Two discs with Rolf Ericson, Gosta Theselius, Jack Noren. Sweden; 1950; private.
- *Bird with Strings* (Columbia 34832). With strings, Al Haig, Roy Haynes, Candido. New York; 1951; broadcast.
- *Live at Christy's* (Charlie Parker P10-402). With Benny Harris, Wardell Gray, Dick Twardzik, Charles Mingus. Massachusetts; 1951; broadcast.
- *Summit Meeting at Birdland* (Columbia 34831). With Dizzy Gillespie, Bud Powell, Tommy Potter, Roy Haynes, Milt Buckner, John Lewis, Kenny Clarke. New York; 1951–53; broadcast.
- *Bird Flies with the Herd* (Main Man 617). With the Woody Herman Orchestra (Clifford Brown). Missouri; 1951; private.
- *On the Coast* (Jazz Showcase 5007). With the Harry Babasin All Stars, Sonny Criss, Chet Baker. California; 1952; private.
- *Live at the Rockland Palace* (Charlie Parker 502). Two discs with Walter Bishop, Mundell Lowe, Teddy Kotick, Max Roach, strings. New York; 1952; private.
- *Duke Ellington Concert at Carnegie Hall* (Vee Jay DJD 28023). Two discs with strings, Dizzy Gillespie, Roy Haynes (Ellington, Stan Getz, Billie Holiday). New York; 1952; broadcast.
- *One Night in Washington* (Musician p-11184). With The Orchestra. Washington D.C.; 1953; private.
- *Charlie Parker* (Queen-disc 002). With Kenny Dorham, Bill Harris, Lucky Thompson, Bud Powell, Charles Mingus, Max Roach. New York; 1949–53; broadcast.
- *Charlie Parker at Storyville* (Blue Note BT 85108). With Herb Pomeroy, Red Garland, Sir Charles Thompson, Roy Haynes, Kenny Clarke. Massachusetts; 1953; broadcast.
- *Jazz at Massey Hall* (Debut 124). With Dizzy Gillespie, Bud Powell, Charles Mingus, Max Roach. Toronto; 1953; private.
- *New Bird: Hi Hat Broadcasts* (Phoenix 10). With Herbie Williams, Rollins Griffith. Massachusetts; 1953; broadcast.
- *New Bird Volume 2* (Phoenix Jazz 12). With Herbie Williams, Rollins Griffith, Dizzy Gillespie, Dick Hyman. Massachusetts, New York; 1952–54; broadcast.
- *Kenton and Bird* (Jazz Supreme 703). With the Stan Kenton Orchestra (Dizzy Gillespie). California; 1954; broadcast.
- *Birdland All Stars at Carnegie Hall* (Roulette 127). Two discs with John Lewis, Percy Heath, Kenny Clarke (Count Basie, Billie Holiday, Lester Young, Sarah Vaughan). New York; 1954; private.

A Selected Bibliography

Amram, David. *Vibrations*. New York: Macmillan, 1968.

Balliett, Whitney. "Bird." *The New Yorker*, March 1, 1976.

Brown, Tony. "Interview with Baroness de Koenigswarter." *Melody Maker*, February 16, 1957.

Chambers, Jack. *Milestones 1*. New York: Beech Tree/Morrow, 1983.

Collier, James Lincoln. *The Making of Jazz*. New York: Houghton Mifflin Company, 1978.

Dance, Stanley. *The World of Count Basie*. New York: Scribners, 1980.

Dance, Stanley. *The World of Earl Hines*. New York: Scribners, 1977.

Dexter, Dave Jr. *The Jazz Story*. New York: Prentice-Hall, 1964.

Dufty, Maely Daniele. "The 'Bird' Has Flown But Not the Vultures." *New York Citizen Call*, July 23, 1960.

Ellison, Ralph. *Shadow and Act*. New York: Random House, 1964.

Feather, Leonard. *Inside Jazz*. New York: Robbins, 1949.

Feather, Leonard. "Yardbird Flies Home." *Metronome*, August 1947.

Feather, Leonard. "Parker Finally Finds Peace." *Down Beat*, April 10, 1955.

Giddins, Gary. *Riding on a Blue Note*. New York: Oxford University Press, 1981.

Gillespie, Dizzy with Al Fraser. *To Be or Not to Bop*. New York: Doubleday, 1979.

Gitler, Ira. *Jazz Masters of the 40's*. New York: Macmillan, 1966.

Harrison, Max. *Charlie Parker*. New York: A. S. Barnes, 1961.

Hentoff, Nat. *Jazz Is*. New York: Random House, 1976.

Hodier, Andre. *Jazz: Its Evolution and Essence*. New York: Grove Press, 1956.

Jones, LeRoi. *Blues People*. New York: William Morrow, 1963.

Karner, Gary. "Interview with Pepper Adams, Part 2." *Cadence*, February 1986.

Keepnews, Orrin. "Charlie Parker." Shapiro, Nat, and Hentoff, Nat. *The Jazz Makers*. New York: Rinehart, 1957.

Koster, Piet, and Bakker, Dick M., *Charlie Parker 1940–1955* (four volumes). Holland: Micrography, 1976.

Macdonald, Julie. "Bird Lives!" *Follies*, May 1979.

Mack, Gerald, and Mansfield, Horace, Jr. "Interview with Roy Porter." *Be-Bop and Beyond*, August/September 1985.

Morgenstern, Dan, liner note to *One Night in Birdland*. Columbia 34808, 1977.

Owens, Thomas. *Charlie Parker: Techniques of Improvisation* (two volumes). Ann Arbor: University Microfilms International, 1974.

Parker, Chan, and Paudras, Francis. Paris: *To Bird with Love*. Editions Wizlov, 1981.

Patrick, James. "The Music of Charlie Parker," liner note to *Charlie Parker: The Complete Savoy Sessions*. Savoy 5500, 1978.